NITYANANDA
THE DIVINE PRESENCE

NITYANANDA
THE DIVINE PRESENCE

M.U. Hatengdi

WITH A FOREWORD BY
SWAMI CHETANANANDA

RUDRA PRESS • Portland, Oregon

RUDRA PRESS
P.O. Box 13390
Portland, OR 97213-0390
Telephone: 1-800-876-7798
© 1984 M.U. Hatengdi

Edited by Aurelia Navarro
Designed by Deborah Carpenter

Cover painting: Wendell Field
Photographs: M.D. Suvarna

Library of Congress Cataloging-in-Publication Data

Hatengdi, M. U., 1914 -
   Nityananda: the divine presence / M.U. Hatengdi; with a foreword
by Swami Chetanananda. — 1st ed.
      p.   cm.
   Includes index
   ISBN 0-915801-00-0
   1. Nityananda, Swami, 1897-1961.
BL1175.N48H37   1990
294.5'513'092 — dc20   90-19465
[B]   CIP

94 95 96 97 10 9 8 7 6 5 4 3

*The great incarnate monist Shankara,
on composing the paean Soundarya Lahari in
praise of the Universal Mother, wrote that it was
like waving a light before the Sun made of its own flame,
like offering oblation to the Moon from the drops oozing
out of the Moonstone, or like satisfying the Ocean
with its own water. Similarly this little tribute
was rendered possible by his own Grace.*

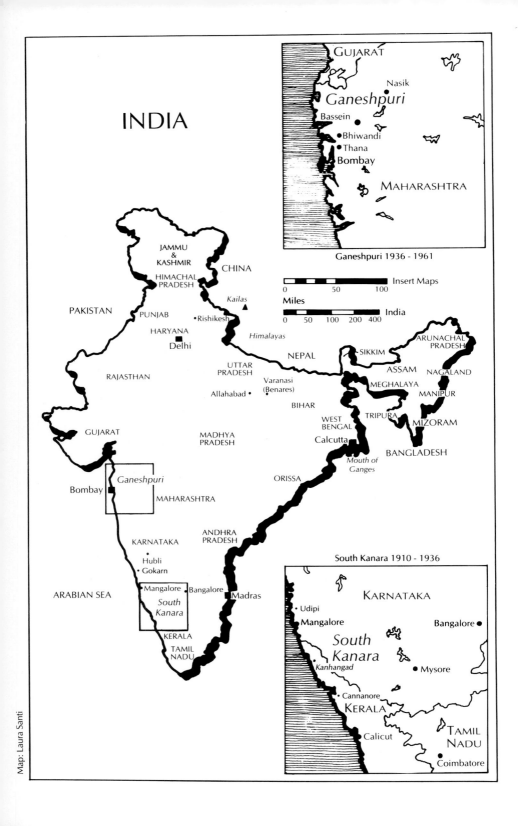

INDIA

GUJARAT

Nasik

Ganeshpuri

Bassein

Bhiwandi

Thana

Bombay

MAHARASHTRA

Ganeshpuri 1936 - 1961

JAMMU & KASHMIR

CHINA

HIMACHAL PRADESH

Kailas

PAKISTAN

PUNJAB

•Rishikesh

HARYANA

Delhi

Himalayas

NEPAL

SIKKIM

ARUNACHAL PRADESH

UTTAR PRADESH

ASSAM

NAGALAND

RAJASTHAN

Varanasi (Benares)

MEGHALAYA

MANIPUR

Allahabad •

BIHAR

TRIPURA

MIZORAM

GUJARAT

MADHYA PRADESH

WEST BENGAL

Calcutta

BANGLADESH

Ganeshpuri

ORISSA

Mouth of Ganges

Bombay

MAHARASHTRA

Insert Maps

0   50   100

Miles

India

0   50 100 200 400

KARNATAKA

ANDHRA PRADESH

Hubli

• Gokarn

Mangalore

Bangalore

Madras

South Kanara

KERALA

TAMIL NADU

ARABIAN SEA

South Kanara 1910 - 1936

KARNATAKA

• Udipi

Mangalore

Bangalore •

South Kanara

Kanhangad

• Mysore

• Cannanore

KERALA

TAMIL NADU

Calicut

Coimbatore •

Map: Laura Santi

Contents

Foreword

*Swami Chetanananda, an American meditation master in the lineage of
Nityananda, is Abbot of the Rudrananda Ashram and Director of the Nityananda
Institute in Cambridge, Massachusetts.* The Rudrananda Ashram is a community
of people living a practical spiritual life. Its teaching and meditation practice are
derived from the ancient Kashmir Shaivite traditions. The Ashram is named for
Swami Rudrananda, an American spiritual teacher who was deeply influenced by
his contacts with Nityananda and who was initiated into the Saraswati order of
monks by Swami Muktananda. Swami Chetanananda assumed leadership of the
Ashram on Rudrananda's passing in 1973. The Nityananda Institute is a not-for-
profit center for meditation and quality living committed to making a spiritual life
both understandable and accessible to Americans. It is named in loving gratitude
for Nityananda of Ganeshpuri who inspired our teachers.*

During a trip to India in 1973, I visited the *samadhi* shrine (*Samadhi
Mandir*) of Nityananda. To reach the coutryside town of Ganeshpuri
where Nityananda lived for over 30 years and established an Ashram,
I hired a taxi. The driver assured me that he knew the way to
Ganeshpuri well; he had been there several times himself. When he
learned that this was my first visit, he told the following story.

As a young man he had heard that a very great saint lived in
Ganeshpuri, and decided to go there to receive his blessing. On arriving, he had to get into a line several hours long—at this point in
Nityananda's life thousands of people came daily to see him. The line
moved slowly forward. As he came near enough to see Nityananda, he
observed that the latter spoke little. One by one each person in the line

ix

* *The Nityananda Institute moved to Portland, Oregon in 1993.*

would bow to the saint, offer a gift, or ask a question. Nityananda replied simply, sometimes with only a gesture or sound. Thus, when the driver's turn came, he was quite startled to hear Nityananda say *"Go and bring your brother here."* He was also deeply touched, because he had heard of the healing powers of Nityananda, and his brother had been blind since birth.

The following week the two men returned to Ganeshpuri. Nityananda told the driver to leave his brother and return for him in three days. When he returned three days later, his brother could see.

I had the good fortune in India to hear many stories about Nityananda—stories that reflected his simplicity, his austerity, his detachment from the world, and his pure, powerful love for those who came to him. The more stories I heard, the more I recognized two things: First, that these stories deserved a larger audience—that they could be useful and inspiring to people in the West as well as in India; and second, that stories about Nityananda were the most powerful and direct way to express the flavor of his extraordinary presence. I decided to gather as many stories as I could, and began by traveling along the route that Nityananda followed, from Cannanore in the south, through Mangalore and Kanhangad and finally to Ganeshpuri. Along the way, I met many people who had known him or whose parents had known him. Their remarkable, moving narratives confirmed my sense of what an exceptional being Nityananda was, and how rich a collection of stories about his life could be.

The actions of saints or gurus are often bewildering to both their followers and the people who hear of them. Their words may be confusing, their actions might seem peculiar, their knowledge and insight contrary to the precepts of logic—all of these things cause consternation and sometimes doubt. This is true in the lives of all great spiritual beings, from Jesus to the Buddha to Mohammed and Moses. There is infinite mystery surrounding the actions of such people. Yet, always their followers and devotees have wanted to capture the inexpressible presence of their gurus; to inspire others with examples of their detachment and wisdom. So they tell stories.

Nityananda's life is no exception to this rule. Much of what he did was enigmatic. Many of his behaviors startled even his closest devotees. And yet, everything he touched was uplifted. Whether indirectly, or after many years had passed, or through circumstances that could never have been predicted—Nityananda's actions benefitted the seeker, even those who came with base motives. Story after story testifies to this.

In 1979 and 1980, I was collecting these stories of Nityananda with the help of Swami Prajnananda, Swami Muktananda's assistant, who gave me great encouragement and provided a list of contacts. I heard then about Captain Hatengdi and the book he had written. Because the Captain had been a devotee of Nityananda for many years he not only had recollections of his own to relate, but also knew of many others who had had direct experience of Nityananda. When I visited with him in Bombay, I recognized that with his help, I had an extraordinary opportunity to accomplish what I had set out to do. Together we agreed to publish the book you now hold in your hands.

Two years later, through the work of the editorial staff at the Nityananda Institute, this book is available to the public. The stories that follow paint a portrait of a man who was remarkable in every aspect. It is an intimate portrait; one feels on reading them that one could easily have been there. As far as it is possible to reveal mystery, they reveal his mystery, as far as it is possible to capture grace, they capture his grace, as far as it is possible to put words to the Divine, they testify to his divinity. It is with sincere pleasure and gratitude that we present this book.

Swami Chetanananda

Preface

After I had written a few articles on the great Master of Ganeshpuri, friends who were also devotees from the early days pressed me to attempt writing his life story. Mrs. M. Krishnabai was the first to urge me to undertake this service to the greatest Master of all time. However, I could not gather as much information and assistance as needed to fulfill this ideal of a biography of Nityananda. Instead, only a few well authenticated incidents have been recorded. There are certain to be many omissions. Readers who wish to offer information for inclusion in a possible future edition are requested to write. Similarly, if there are errors or if the narrative contains a misrepresentation of facts, I sincerely apologize and would revise the record in the next edition if the account is proved to be factually incorrect.

My project was aided by a chance meeting with Mr. R. B. Bellare of Bandra in September, 1980. Without his unstinting zeal, efficiency and regularity, motivated only by his desire to contribute his dedicated effort, this little tribute to the Master would not have been possible.

I believe this is the first attempt to present Nityananda in an authentic setting to the English speaking public. Later, it may be presented to others through suitable translations. I was particularly gratified by the interest of Swami Chetanananda of the United States and by the Swamiji's proposal to have it published there.

In this regard, I wish to thank Sharon Ward and Aurelia Navarro at the Nityananda Institute of Cambridge, Massachusetts, for their dedicated effort and unflagging zeal in editing my original manuscript in order to present Nityananda to the American reader in clear, understandable language, without any unnecessary frills.

My aim will be more than fulfilled if this book aids the reader, to even the smallest extent, in exploring and experiencing the wonder of the Master known as Nityananda.

M.U. Hatengdi
July, 1981

NITYANANDA

THE DIVINE PRESENCE

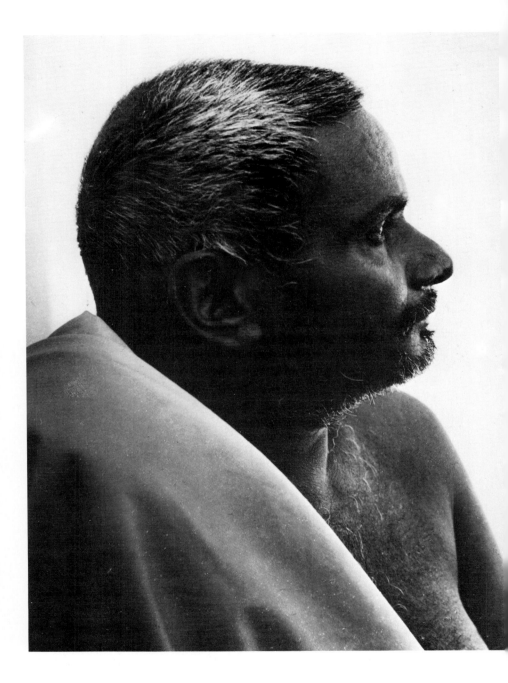

Introduction

Behind Nityananda's awe-inspiring presence was the heart of a compassionate mother. Already a full-fledged Master in his teens and twenties, he may have been speaking of himself when he compared *sadhus* (seekers of truth)* to jackfruits, whose forbidding exteriors nonetheless yield honeyed sweetness when penetrated with skill. From his earliest known days to his last ones in Ganeshpuri, the Master's mere presence provided a sense of security for the poor and for those in distress, and hope for spiritual aspirants. People from all walks of life came for his *darshan*—*yogis, sanyasis,* scholars, musicians, *shankaracharyas,* politicians, ministers, saints, sinners, actors, the rich and the poor, the sick and the strong. They came from all parts of the country, and abroad as well.

Yet, much of his life is not clearly known; even though there are many stories, these often place him in widely separated places at the same time, leading to considerable confusion about his true age or background. Devotees always listened carefully for any clues or details of his youth and early years, and occasionally Nityananda would touch upon an incident from the past in his casual conversation; however, he would cut short any attempt to obtain details. If one persisted, a severe admonition was the only result. Thus, he made passing reference to visiting Ceylon and Singapore, and displayed an intimate knowledge of the Himalayan regions. It is said he spoke of being in

---

A complete Glossary of all Sanskrit terms follows the text. The terms are italicized the first time they appear and are often followed by a brief definition in parentheses.

Madras in 1902 when Swami Vivekananda attained *samadhi* (left his earthly body); yet, his apparent age in the twenties would imply that he had been an infant at the time Vivekananda passed away.

Even his name is an area of mystery. Stories of his childhood say he was called Ram by his adoptive mother; the name Nityananda, which means eternal bliss, became attached to him as a description of the state of mind he inspired. To a devotee who sat before him ecstatically repeating "nityanand, nityanand" as if it were a mantra, the Master said, *"Is it a name? It is a state."* Thus many of the early devotees called him Swami, Master, or sadhu, while the name Nityananda became attached to him only in later years.

Clearly, painting a portrait of a Master such as Nityananda requires not only a large canvas but also an expert artist; that painting is not yet done. Of the hundreds of thousands who came to have darshan, few were moved to record or translate their experiences for the benefit of others. Further, Nityananda had no gospel and prescribed no special readings or *sadhana* (spiritual practice or discipline). Advice given to one person was not necessarily the same as that given to another. He simply urged all devotees to cultivate a pure mind and an intense desire for liberation (*shuddha bhavana* and *shraddha*).

His self-abnegation was complete. He dressed in nothing but a loincloth (*langoti*), sometimes not even that. During the time he was in South Kanara, he ate only if fed. He had a total disregard for the elements or for his nightly resting place. "Miracles" occurred naturally all around him, including phenomenal cures from ailments. Yet he was never motivated by any desire for publicity or for winning devotees. He frowned on any attempt to publicize him and admonished devotees who attributed to him experiences that could be described as miracles. When pressed for an explanation, he would say that it was the greatness of the place, or the faith of the people involved. Or he would say that, when its time came, the event occurred by the power of God.

Everything that happens,
happens automatically by the will of God.

As a great powerhouse and a transmitting center, he desired only that people develop their powers of reception toward what he was capable of transmitting. He would say: *"The ocean has plenty of water, it is the size of the container brought to collect it that determines the quantity taken."* Being an embodiment of the ideal and the pure, he would say, *"One who sees this one* [1] [Nityananda] *once will not forget,"* implying that the seed of spiritual consciousness sown by the darshan would sprout in due course when cultivated correctly. By his own statement he had no earthly *guru* nor had to perform any sadhana as such, and he adopted no disciples as he had no intention of establishing an organization. His devotees were legion, but most of them were common householders. His mission, silent and unseen, was to provide relief to suffering humanity, whether people came to him or not, and to transmit a wider consciousness to those who sought higher values. His grace emanated from his aura and from his silent companionship. Even a glimpse of his resplendent personality was adequate to shatter the ego of the proud, or to evoke the hope and aspirations of the genuine seeker.

Even those who sought him for material success benefitted and the few who came for pure devotion found their evolutionary processes accelerated with little or no effort on their part. Nityananda did this transforming process by becoming an obsession, if one may express it that way, a divine obsession. Although devotees lived in the everyday world, they imbibed the spirit of the *Bhagavad Gita*, and were gradually processed from within, without much striving. In this way, seekers and other pilgrims would benefit, both through the rousing of their spiritual consciousness and by meeting life's challenges in a capable manner through the Master's help. By converting their very breath into consciousness, there was a gradual ripening from within, leading to a longing and a restlessness for the divine, and a dispassion for the things of the world without affecting efficiency in one's chosen field. That is how his grace silently worked.

He was a mighty spiritual force that filled the South Kanara district for a few years and then rolled on to Kanhangad, Gokarn and Vajreshwari, and later settled at Ganeshpuri, nestled at the foot of the majestic Mandakini mountain, amidst light blue hills, green pastures, hot springs, and the Bhimeshwar shrine. Perhaps Nityananda had been moved to choose this place in order to revive the holiness of this ancient spiritual center. [2]

---

[1] He never referred to himself in the first person singular. He would say "this one" or "from here."

[2] Legend has it that Sage Vashista (Sri Rama's guru) chose this place for a very special sacrifical rite (*yajna*). He created 360 hot springs so that the large number of invited sages could bathe in a different spring each day of the year, in order to ward off physical ailments and mental distractions

(cont'd)

Nityananda used to say that the true reward for genuine devotion *(bhakti)* was a greater dose of pure desireless devotion, not material prosperity or social success. Great Masters such as Nityananda play the role of the eternal *Gopala*, tending the allegorical flock of devotees, guiding and watching them at pasture during their earthly sojourn, helping them onward, then bringing them home safely as the evening closes on their lives, either to rest permanently in liberation *(mukti)* if they are advanced enough, or to start afresh by leading them again through another morning of birth—and so on, in a continual process of evolution.

Nityananda was widely known in South India, yet even among those who had the good fortune to recognize him as their teacher only a few sought the right thing from him. They are indeed the fortunate ones. Although Masters such as Nityananda are capable of granting many things, there is truly only one thing to be sought from them. In Nityananda's own words: *"One must seek the shortest way and the fastest means to get back home—to turn the spark within into a blaze, to be merged in and to identify with that greater fire which ignited the spark."*

---

brought about by the agencies of Indra who for some reason had decided to thwart the sacrificial rites. Finding that Vashista was managing all right despite these obstructions, Indra finally seemed to have aimed his Vajra-Astra to destroy it. Mother Parvati reportedly presented herself and absorbed the weapon and thus saved the yajna. Hence she was installed at the spot as Vajreshwari and a shrine was erected for her. The present fort-like structure was constructed by the Peshwas. In their prayers to her, they pledged that if they succeeded in capturing the Bassein Fort from the Portugese, they would raise a new temple to her on the old site, patterned after a fort.

SHREE
SWAMI NITYANAND

Days of Peace and Happiness

Though Nityananda was in the same part of Southern India as I (Mangalore, South Kanara, and Kanhangad) till the early thirties, it did not occur to me then to seek him out, even though I had seen him on several occasions in Mangalore prior to 1925. [3] It was not until about 1939 that I felt the desire for a spiritual teacher. At that time, Nityananda was mentioned by a friend, but neither of us knew exactly where he was or how to get there. However, as my desire intensified, my cousin, whose parents used to visit Ganeshpuri whenever they traveled to Bombay, arranged an opportunity for me. On June 10, 1943 I accompanied them to Nityananda's Ashram and had my first real darshan of him, with the sole intent of meeting him as my spiritual Master. It evoked in me a feeling similar to being reunited with a long-lost relative, accompanied by a special sense of inner security. Though

---

[3] In fact in 1920 (when I was five) Nityananda came to my neighborhood in Mangalore. I saw him in the cattleshed of the house of the late Col. V. R. Mirajkar of Bombay and Lahore, a famous surgeon whose mother was devoted to the young Master. The Colonel recounted that on his return to Mangalore in 1921 after eight years abroad he had argued with his mother. He had been astounded that anyone who was as firm about cleanliness as his mother would tolerate Nityananda. At that time he was a rail-thin young man looking barely a day out of his teens who would sit or lie down any place, from the doormat and dunghill to the cattle-shed and even the dry lavatories, just to avoid crowds. The Colonel added that his mother, an imperious lady, had told him to mind his own business. He regretted having to add that decades passed before he himself recognized Nityananda's greatness.

9

people were often nervous on first meeting him, I was not affected that way despite his taciturnity that morning. Some time later that day, I approached him as he stood on the little porch outside his room (at that time, the space outside the room was not covered) and asked him three questions. I received suitable answers; but as the last question was concerned with mundane matters, the answer was slightly admonitory, implying that I should have known better.

After this first visit to Ganeshpuri in June 1943, I visited the Master every Sunday for a few weeks. During one of these first visits, a young man ran to catch up with me near the Ashram. He asked me where the Ashram was, and whether he could go there. I replied that I believed the Ashram was open to all. He joined me in the room away from the *kunds* (hot springs), and we sat facing the open ground. Nityananda was not in the Ashram. In a short while, we saw the Master approaching from the direction of the river and heard him shout, apparently at the stranger. On entering the Ashram, the Master shouted again and asked the startled man who he had come with. The visitor said he had come with me. The Master drove him away, then came and asked me whether I had brought him. When I replied in the negative, he said *"No talking to anyone here; people come with different predilections* (vasanas)." Although my strict compliance with this directive brought me some trouble subsequently, nonetheless, I felt I was blessed by being unknown, as otherwise I might have been distracted from my main objective in seeking the Master.

During these early visits, the Master was often missing from the Ashram at the time of my arrival; often it was as much as an hour before he would appear from the river side. I was always a little disconcerted until I saw him, since there were rarely others about and the place would feel quite empty. Since I did not know then of his frequent and sudden disappearances from Mangalore and Udipi in the early days, I thought perhaps he traveled to Kanhangad periodically. Thus, on one occasion when he again did not appear until about an hour after my arrival, I asked him whether he had been going to Kanhangad. He immediately replied, *"No going anywhere in future; here only."* As if to put me off any further queries he added, *"Moreover, traveling these days is difficult."* (This was during the second World War, when civilians were advised to travel only when they must.) After this incident, I never missed seeing him in the Ashram. He was always present when I arrived, either on the cement platform or in his room, and occasionally standing near the window in front of it.

The years from 1944 to 1948 were my best years in Caneshpuri. Fortunately I was stationed near Bombay during this period and could spend one golden weekend a month with the Master. Many of these weekends were spent alone with him, particularly till the middle of 1947. He always greeted me rather affectionately, with a two syllable Konkani word meaning "Have you come?"

Certain patterns developed during these visits. For instance, he would always point to the room I should occupy. There were only two, one to the left and the other to the right of his own. The peculiarity was that I would be asked to occupy the rooms by turns; there was never a mistake. My activities also followed a pattern: first I would have my bath in the kunds, and then I would sit to the left of the entrance next to the wooden sill. Invariably in all the 40 or 50 weekends I spent there, the Master would sit in front of me on the first step with the narrow wooden sill separating me from him, thereby blocking my view completely. He would never sit on the right-hand side in which case we could both see each other. The Master would sit for half an hour or more right in front of me and then go round only to return and sit there again. This went on throughout the waking hours during most of my visits. Mostly they were silent sessions. In the beginning, the moment he came and sat near me I would feel drowsy, and I had to use all my self-control to remain awake, but gradually I got over this feeling. I did not know what it meant, but I had a feeling that sitting near him was as good as entering into a meditational exercise and hence the drowsiness.

Punctually at 10:00 at night, he would ask me to retire and close the doors. With the doors closed and the little kerosene bed lamp put out, there was total darkness. During the monsoon, there would be a jungle serenade of frogs and crickets with the glow worms lighting up the trees in rhythmic regularity. During all my visits the Master would slowly push open my door at exactly 4:00 in the morning and stand at the entrance. Though there seemed no possibility of my waking up at that hour, I would open my eyes each time he stood there in the darkness; as soon as I opened my eyes, he would say, "*It's 4:00,*" then just close the door and walk away. I would immediately get up, have a bath and then return to my place near the entrance of the room. He would join me for some coffee usually black but slightly sweetened with *ghee* (a kind of clarified butter) instead of milk which was scarce. There was much affection shown during these visits particularly when we were by ourselves from these morning coffee sessions onward. These were weekends of great peace and happiness for me, which created a longing for his company, an eager waiting for the monthly weekend to come again.

Being in the Master's presence led to a feeling of security and a sense that he was watching over you; there are many stories of the Master's far-ranging vision and protection. For me, one small incident from 1946 illustrated this perfectly. It was an early morning near the end of the monsoon season. It was dark and the grounds were wet, slippery, and treacherous. On my way to the baths, I fell and cut my leg on the sharp stones, causing considerable pain as well as copious bleeding. I washed the wound with rain water until I thought the bleeding had stopped, then went for my bath. Back in my room I was trying to evaluate the wound when the Master suddenly appeared, poured a little sandalwood oil exactly on the injured place and went away as briskly as he had come, all without a word.

Indeed, most of my periods with the Master were spent in silence, though there were occasions when he would speak a few words. The words he said at the close of my third visit were significant. He said that when one obstacle was overcome, another would present itself, until the experience was complete and the mind was equal to face any situation, with the correct perspective on life. These ideas disheartened me a bit then; I was young and still nursed a number of worldly ambitions. To view life as an obstacle course did not seem a happy prospect. Yet I knew that I had sought him for spiritual, not worldly, development and thus there could be no ultimate disappointment. Already I was blessed with a strong inner sense of security and a longing to receive more of his grace.

When the Master did speak, his speech was often casual and tangential, almost in the nature of an *obiter dictum*. For instance, the silence one night was broken by the solitary sentence that whatever Jesus said could also be found in the *Gita*. Of course I was quite ignorant of this at the time.

Often it was not until years later that I appreciated the true significance of what I had taken to be casual utterances. This happened even in two very important matters of my personal life. I did not mentally accept his pronouncements because they had been casually stated. Only years later did I realize that his words *had* to be fulfilled.

Both in 1947 and 1956 I worked against what I thought were his casual opinions, but they had to be fulfilled, even though one case involved the negation of a Government recommendation and choice. In the other instance also, many unbelievable developments had to take place to fulfill these apparently casual expressions. Recently I heard that when the Master was asked how to know if one was a *jnani* (one who has attained divine wisdom), he said that the words of a jnani are always and automatically fulfilled.

Another interesting conversation with the Master took place in 1944. I was feeling that I was not performing any sadhana as such and this inadequacy was tormenting me. At the same time, I was afraid to ask him what practice I should undertake, lest some severe discipline be prescribed like breathing exercises, or intoning mantras. One night when we were sitting together I diffidently asked whether I should read anything. (I knew that I could always undertake reading.) The reply came instantly: *"Not necessary—not necessary—if you must read, read the* Gita.*"*

While the Master was generally disinterested in matters of politics, he was quite thoroughly informed of all occurrences, as the following incidents indicate. Two days after Mountbatten took over as Viceroy I arrived at the Ashram on my monthly weekend. The Master sat near me and said, *"Mountbatten is a good naval officer but he has no experience of politics."* Today, an objective historian could perhaps find material to support this view.

When Independence was only four weeks away, that Saturday night Nityananda made some weighty pronouncements about our future. First he said *"What does* swaraj *mean?"* Having defined it as freedom or self-rule, he hinted that there was still a little time to go for real swaraj and that the training received so far was not complete, hinting at the same time that there would be considerable begging and suffering. The Konkani word for begging can also mean "requesting" depending on the context. In this case it would appear the Master meant that there would be continuing dependence on outside assistance which would perforce limit freedom. He added that the matter was being hastened by interested parties like a fruit being ripened before its time.

I did not understand him then as the potentialities were great and euphoria high. I remember even foreigners telling me that we were

lucky, with so much horsepower that one had only to press the ac-
celerator. Alas, the reality of today falls short of the hopes and ideals of
that time; perhaps for this also *"the time is not yet."* Indeed, the Master
envisaged the division of the country into several states followed by
petty rivalries and jealousies. All that he said has come to pass.

A couple of months later (in September 1947) during my monthly
visit, I again heard the Master speak in relation to a great national
leader. When I heard these words, the Master was speaking as if in answer to a request from someone standing before him. He implied that
there was not much time left for this leader and asked whether he was
not yet satisfied with his name, fame and achievements and why he
should not retire from politics, close his eyes and think of God, for God
would come to him (implying that he was spiritually an advanced
soul). He added that one man, however great, cannot do everything;
life should be treated like a relay race with each person covering the bit
of track meant for him as fast as he could and then passing the baton.
Four months later Mahatma Gandhi was assassinated under circumstances the Master had spoken of to devotees.

From the spiritual point of view the statement that interested me
most came from the Master sometime in June 1945. It was a very dark
night, and I was at my usual place near the door in the room nearest to
the baths. On this odd night the Master was sitting behind me some 12
feet away; we both faced south, peering into the darkness. Suddenly
there was a loud shout from the Master: *"Who's that?"* I had to strain
my eyes to see a person slowly moving up near our room. The Master
had addressed him in Konkani. The man replied by merely saying "I."
Another shout came from behind me: *"I means who?"* This question
was repeated. The man did not reply but came to the entrance of the
room and put a plate on the step just next to me. *"What's that?"* shouted
the Master. The man replied *"Satyanarayana prasad."* [4] The Master
shouted back: *"Whose prasad for whom?"* After repeating this a second time, he added, *"Is anything known about this place* [i.e. him-
self]?" Having already accepted the Master intuitively as an incarnate

---

[4]Satyanarayana is a name of Vishnu; there is a popular ritual known by this name which is
performed in order to attain certain desired results.

personality when I first had his darshan in June 1943, this only strengthened my personal belief. Nevertheless I wondered why he should appear angry, and slowly turned to look at him. I saw him sitting in a posture radiating power and quickly turned away to gaze into the darkness again. Immediately he affectionately addressed me saying: *"Prasad means something received with God presenting himself fully satisfied in the chosen form and bestowing the gift. You may have it now."* I understood that it had now been rendered prasad by his having asked me to take it. He then added, *"That man has not come for prasad. He has done this in the other ashram with a sankalpa."* (A sankalpa is a resolution taken to perform some action if a prayer is answered. Nityananda generally discouraged such vows.) Soon the man began to narrate his story. The Master however admonished him and told him to return for the night to the ashram from which he had come.

One night in October 1945, the Master was sitting in front of me and suddenly said: *"The mother is more important. The mother knows; the father only believes. It is the mother who points out the father to the child, and the child believes her without questioning; it is also she who points out brothers and sisters. What the mother is to the child, the guru is to the disciple. Just as the mother points out the father to the child, so also the guru reveals God to the disciple, and enables him to experience His presence."* I must confess I had never thought of these things in the manner now presented to me. It seemed so simple and yet so true.

One morning in 1946 when we were sitting in our usual places near the entrance, a man entered. The Master got up at once, removed a stick from the roof, struck him four or five times, replaced the stick, and sat near me. The man went away without having uttered a sound. Knowing I was confused, the Master said to me: *"This one has not beaten him. They come to get beaten."* One is reminded of the Nadi-grantha reading given in Appendix A. Many persons believed that with such beating they were blessed and their troubles averted.

There were quite a few occasions when the Master disowned responsibility for his actions—benevolent or apparently not so benevolent. One might recall the story of Vyasa, the great sage who wrote the *Vedas*, the eighteen *Puranas*, and the *Mahabharata*, (including the

Gita), and in whose honor the *Guru Purnima* is observed every July. He was sitting on the banks of the river Jumna one evening when some shepherd girls with pots of curds approached, wishing to cross the river. Since it was getting dark and the river was at full tide, they asked the sage to use his good offices to make the river provide a passage for them. He asked if there was anything to eat, and accepted the offered curds. After eating, he addressed the river: "If I have not eaten anything make a way for these girls." The river immediately complied. Because the real Vyasa was continually identified only with the soul (*atman*) inside, the real Vyasa had not eaten. In the Nadigrantha reading in Appendix A, the Master is also described as being "always with the atman—not in the body."

From 1948 to 1954 I had only two or three contacts with the Master, and I was already a stranger to the new generation of devotees. From 1955 to 1957 I was in Bombay again but I often felt lost in the crowd during these monthly visits. I usually came only for the day, and if I did stay overnight, I stayed in the big hall since the two rooms flanking the Master's room were no longer being used by visitors; one had been converted into a kitchen and the other was kept closed.

During one of these monthly visits (in September 1956), I decided to spend the night in Ganeshpuri. Instead of sitting in the hall where I did not know anyone, I decided to sit outside the hall in front of the room then being used as a kitchen. From there I had continuous darshan of the Master on the bench. As the evening deepened, there was a little drizzle. It was already quite dark at about seven when the Master called Panwalla (a devotee I came to know only after this incident) and asked him to open the room near the baths and allot it to me for the night. The room was full of articles gifted to the Master and had not been occupied for a long time. I left early the next morning. I later learned that the Master left the old Ashram for *Kailas* [5] the same morning.

---

[5]*Kailas* was the name by which Nityananda's new Ashram, opened in 1956, was known. The word itself refers to the mythic Himalayan home of the god Shiva.

After 1957, my visits to Ganeshpuri were restricted to one or two a year, and my last visit before the *mahasamadhi*[6] was in October 1960. I had not befriended any of the other devotees visiting the Ashram in compliance (mistaken or otherwise) with the instructions of the Master; this began to tell severely on me during these visits. After the Master shifted his living quarters to Kailas (the new Ashram) in late 1956, specific times were set for darshan. Thus, the old central hall was usually empty as the devotees mostly clustered in the western hall. Hence during my odd trip or two per year during 1957-60, I usually occupied the corner of the old hall very near the bench on which the Master used to sit. It was my habit to arrive in the early afternoon for these visits and to leave by six or seven the next morning. However, to get darshan meant an hourly knock at Kailas until the doors were opened—sometimes at five and sometimes later. Only if one were well acquainted with the devotee attendants inside the Ashram could one be admitted for darshan at other times. While this was occasionally arranged for devotees such as I who came from distant places, as I was largely unknown to this new generation of devotee attendants, I was not often obliged in this way. This created some frustration in me; I wondered why the Master did not give me a place in Kailas for my brief annual visits.

When I ultimately got darshan that evening, the Master asked: *"Where do you stay these days?"* Since he had already given indications that he knew what I was doing even at outstations, I thought it was not fair to pose that question to me. Hence I rather petulantly replied "Where else—there only."In a slightly admonishing tone, with his index finger pointing to the spot I occupied in the old Ashram, he replied, *"That alone is good—that alone is good."* I must confess that I did not accept it at the time, because I was thinking that if that were so, why should he be in Kailas? But I kept silent. It was only after the mahasamadhi, when his holy remains were interred at almost the exact spot that I occupied during these visits, that I came to appreciate what he said then.

My last visit to Ganeshpuri while the Master was in his human form was during October 1960. An attendant devotee opened the door late

---

[6] Literally, the great resolving; in this usage, the conscious shedding of the physical body.

in the evening after several hourly knocks, and asked me to sit in front of the platform next to the easy chair. The Master was resting on the inner platform and some devotee was rendering *seva* (selfless service). About ten minutes passed. Two other devotees in the passage were trying to play the voice of the Master on a new tape recorder. The particular words they had managed to catch were being heard. The Master was saying repeatedly, *"Without the grace of the guru, nothing happens."* I was trying to apply this to myself and wondering whether my waiting for darshan for five long hours, with an hourly knock and retirement back to the hall, was due to lack of grace, and if so what exactly I had done to merit this treatment. As soon as this thought came, the Master abruptly arose from the platform inside, briskly came out and lay on the platform in front of and facing me. There was no light on the platform but there was one just above where I sat; he kept staring at me and I had to keep shifting my gaze. No words were exchanged. After about 15 minutes, he went again to the inner platform.

I was disturbed by the proportions his body had assumed. I felt I would not be able to breathe with that waistline. My wonder was the greater because I knew of his food habits. It was only years later that I was told that other devotees had also noticed and inquired about this, with the Master tailoring different answers for different persons, as would suit them.

That evening when I told the attendant devotee that I would be leaving early the next morning, he asked me to meet him at the baths at 4 A.M., then enter the main hall of Kailas with him and have darshan at six. When I came in at six, I found the Master sleeping on the inner platform with his face turned toward the wall. Not knowing how long I would have to wait, I went to his platform and bent over to see his face. He opened his left eye and nodded to indicate that I could go. Not a single word was exchanged during this last visit. Even though I had become an infrequent visitor since 1948, I had always received at least a greeting from the Master. This was the first time (and on my last visit) that silence reigned supreme. I was perhaps expected to have graduated into silence. I had not. I was left with a feeling that there would still be a struggle ahead of me, and this was so. Nevertheless even to dwell on the golden weekends I spent sitting near him brought and still brings feelings of peace and unaccountable happiness.

Early Years

Nityananda used to say that as long as his human form existed it did not matter how and where it came from, implying that it was idle curiosity to probe into such limiting factors. However, devotees who had the rare privilege of rendering service to the Master in his later years have gathered some details of his birth and early life. Although these stories are not in complete agreement, nevertheless the available information can be woven into a brief yet plausible hypothesis of his early childhood and boyhood days.

It is the turn of the century—late November or early December. The rays of the setting sun slant muted light through the darkness of the thickly wooded area. [7] Two crows on a cashew tree caw loudly as if to attract attention. An elderly *harijan* (untouchable) woman is returning home with dried leaves and twigs for the evening fire. She is the leader of the women in this jungle group. Thinking there may be something useful to bring home, she follows the sound; the crows fly off at her approach.

---

[7] Known as Guruvana , it is a few miles away from the Kanhangad Rock Ashram. The temple at Guruvana is the second temple dedicated to the Master; it was inaugurated in May, 1966 by the late Mr. Silam, then Lt. Governor of Pondicherry.

In a clump of bushes, she discovers a small male infant on the ground. He is carefully wrapped in a white cloth. She has her own family to take care of but seeing the helpless baby, she remembers that Unniamma's mother wants to adopt a child for her barren daughter. Grateful for this opportunity to bring joy to Unniamma, she picks up the infant and carries him to her home. She is carrying the infant Nityananda.

He is lighter-skinned than his rescuers, the color of ripe wheat. After a night in the camp, the old woman wraps him once again in his white cloth and carries him to the village of Unniamma's mother, who accepts the child with great joy. To seal the bargain, she "pays" the harijan woman ten pounds of rice. The child is then taken to Unniamma's village of Pantalayini near Calicut (an area known as Koilande). She works both in the household of Mr. Ishwar Iyer, a local lawyer, and in the neighboring temples. Unniamma gratefully adopts the child, naming him Ram.

When he was about 18 months old, Ram developed liver trouble. Mr. Iyer, who had taken a personal interest in him, saw to it that the child received medical help and was given *Ayurvedic* (ancient Hindu art of healing) medicines. Despite these efforts, the boy's condition worsened; he grew very thin while his stomach became more and more distended. Often he would cry all night. Unniamma's landlord lost patience with the family; on many occasions when he was awakened by the crying, he would shout at Unniamma to throw Ram in the storm drain.

After one such night, Unniamma was so worried that she could not attend to her duties with Mr. Iyer but instead took the child for a walk. As she was walking with the ailing child, a tall dark-skinned man in foreign clothes walked past. Somehow the distraught mother felt that this was a medicine man from another part of the country, perhaps because of the large satchel slung over his shoulder. She approached him and asked if he could help her child. As if he had been waiting for her, he pulled a packet from his bag, handed it to her and explained that its contents should be mixed with the flesh of a freshly killed crow that had been fried in ghee. A small portion of this should be administered to the child each morning on an empty stomach. She was also told to rub Ram all over with the blood of the crow right after it had been killed.

At this moment, a *toddy tapper*[8] with his morning collection approached. In his right hand he held a crow which he handed over to her. Overjoyed at these sudden developments, she looked around to thank the two men but both had disappeared.

Unniamma immediately started the course of treatment prescribed by the stranger and the child recovered in a remarkably short time. But the application of the crow's blood permanently changed his skin color to a dark bluish hue. When a devotee commented on his black color just a year or two before his mahasamadhi, the Master said that it was not black but blue-black (*Krishnavarna*). Earlier, when the young Nityananda was questioned about his origins or his guru, he would often answer with the cryptic statement that a crow came and the crow left. Not until much later did anyone know about the crow incident that took place in his infancy.

Over the years, Mr. Iyer grew very fond of Ram. A devout man, he was a worshipper of *Bharga*, the divinity of the sun. He felt a strong mystical attraction to Ram; upon the death of Unniamma, Iyer readily took charge of the six-year-old child, taking Ram into his household with paternal affection even though he had children of his own.

Mr. Iyer was a lawyer of local distinction, and many of his younger colleagues from the surrounding villages would come to consult with him. They were surprised to see him, a respected brahmin, attached to a low-caste child such as Ram. But Mr. Iyer saw in Ram much more than a beloved child; to him Ram was a constant friend as well as a stimulating philosopher and a guide in spiritual matters. Ram would always accompany his foster father on his trips to the famous Krishna temple at Guruvayur. On these trips, when the two were alone, Ram's wise explanations of esoteric truths astounded the older man and satisfied his spiritual hunger. If Ram was missing or otherwise not in the house at the proper time, Iyer would be disconsolate and would not attend to his work in the court. One day, a well-known astrologer told Mr. Iyer from his birth chart that the child who had become an addition to his family was an incarnate personality and that Iyer was extremely fortunate to have him as a ward and companion.

However, the young Ram was also quite mischievous and loved to pull pranks, such as taking a deep dive in the neighboring temple tank and then disappearing from view for quite a while, causing considera-

---

[8]The sap of the toddy palm is collected by toddy tappers for the making of a fermented beverage called *arrack*.

ble anxiety. At other times, he would run away after the swim without drying himself, so that Mr. Iyer asked friends and servants to help keep an eye on him. Though he was still a young child, he would be up very early, before four in the morning, and would insist that the other members of the household do likewise, including taking their baths and applying the sacred ash on their foreheads. Although he refused to attend school, he agreed to learn whatever Mr. Iyer could teach him privately. From him he picked up elements of Malayalam, English, Sanskrit, arithmetic and other subjects.

Another of the young Ram's pranks involved the local snake-charmers, who had devised a dishonest money-making scheme. Under cover of darkness, they would release a few cobras in the compound of a selected house. On the following day, they would tell the owner of the danger. But, for a price, they would offer to use their great skill at capturing these dangerous reptiles. In the presence of the owner, they would recall the snakes from their hideouts, proving that relief from the danger had been provided. But when they tried their scheme on Mr. Iyer, the snakes refused to heed their call. The charmers were baffled by their failure until they saw Ram at a distance giggling—he had rendered their mantra ineffective. After a while he allowed them to collect their cobras but cautioned them never to try their tricks again in the Iyer household.

When Ram was about ten years old, Mr. Iyer, knowing he was growing older, decided to undertake a pilgrimage to Benares. [9] He wanted no one but Ram to accompany him. On this trip, which took them to several holy places, young Ram reportedly granted many divine visions to Mr. Iyer. Then, perhaps in Benares, he took leave of the tearful Mr. Iyer although he promised to see him again.

Exactly which centers of pilgrimage the young Master visited and lived in during this time is not known. There is general agreement that he spent these years (from about his 12th to his 16th years) traveling in the North. Several sources indicate that he was well known in the Himalayas as a great *kundalini* yogi.

Ram returned home when he was about 16. He knew that Mr. Iyer's end was near and he returned to fulfill his promise. Mr. Iyer had been thinking about Ram constantly for many days; when he realized that

---

[9] To die in Benares (also known as Kashi and Varanasi) is thought to lead to liberation from the cycle of birth and rebirth.

the boy had really returned, he became ecstatically happy and kept re-peating "nityananda, nityananda" (eternal bliss). This was to become the Master's popular name.

Soon thereafter, Mr. Iyer performed the marriage ceremony of his youngest daughter at Guruvayur. On this occasion, the entire family felt they received the benediction of the deity through Nityananda. As one of the last expressions of his gratitude, Mr. Iyer willed a share of his assets to Nityananda; of course, the Master declined the gift.

During these last days, it is said that the young Nityananda took Mr. Iyer to Udipi on two occasions for the darshan of Ananteshwar and Lord Krishna. (Nityananda's later remark that he was at Udipi when the ancient Ananteshwar temple was under construction—at least 400 years ago—further indicates his earlier association with the place.)

Mr. Iyer fell gravely ill shortly after Nityananda's return. When the end came, he lay resting on Nityananda's lap and expressed the desire to have a vision of Bharga, the divine being residing in the orb of the Sun, the divinity he had worshipped all his life. The young Master granted this request. Shortly afterward, Mr. Iyer entered the abode of lasting peace.

South Kanara

Soon after performing the last rites for Mr. Iyer, Nityananda began his wanderings in the South. The exact places he visited are not known, but just as he wandered in the North after leaving Mr. Iyer in Benares, he now wandered in the South and perhaps a few places in Southeast Asia. From his casual and fragmentary references, it can be assumed that he had been to Ceylon, Rangoon, and Singapore. Nityananda also mentioned being a stowaway on a cargo ship, probably boarding in Madras, and then working on board the ship as a stoker boy. At another time, he spoke of working as a laborer on a rubber estate in Burma. Some thought he had been to Japan, but this is not verified. He once recounted an incident during the First World War when he was forcibly recruited into the Army. He laughed when he told of being taken for a medical examination, and how shocked the doctor was because he could hear no heart beat nor feel any pulse. He discharged Nityananda as medically unfit. Some devotees report that he spoke of being in Madras when Swami Vivekananda went abroad in 1896 and again when he passed away in 1902. Yet Nityananda's appearance would indicate that he was an infant in 1896 and no more than six years old in 1902. But such questioning is immaterial; he was all-knowing. In the mid-fifties, when asked whether he would be going abroad like some of the other Indian swamis, he answered, *"One has to go only if one cannot see places from here or deal with people there."*

The following is one of the few authenticated stories about this time period. The scene is Palani where Lord Subramanya (a brother of Lord Ganesh in Hindu mythology) is the presiding deity. We must visualize the Nityananda of those days: looking like an eccentric vagrant, his body wire-thin as if lashed by severe austerities, but healthy and glowing all the same. Late one morning, he was ascending the last few steps to the sanctum at Palani when the serving priest, having locked the doors of the shrine after morning worship, was coming down. Nityananda asked him to re-open the doors and have an *arathi* (light) waved before the deity. The priest was astonished that a vagrant would dare make such a request of a person of his status and curtly told Nityananda that the time for morning worship was over.

Nityananda went on as if he had not heard. The priest, expecting that Nityananda would walk around the sanctum and offer worship at the Muslim altar at the rear, was not concerned until he heard the temple bells ringing. When he looked back, he was dumbfounded to see the doors of the sanctum open and Nityananda sitting in the place of the deity with an arathi being waved in front of him by invisible hands. The vision vanished in an instant. Then Nityananda came out of the sanctum and stood on one leg for some time, with a steady yogic upward gaze. Apparently, a lot of money was poured at his feet— whether by pilgrims or visitors or some invisible source is not clear. Nityananda, in any case, was accorded all the honors due to a Master. The pilgrims tried to persuade him to stay, but he refused. He gave all the money to the leader of the local sanyasis for a morning meal center (for serving one meal of rice porridge a day to the sanyasis). To complete the story, it was later learned that the local sanyasis had been praying to the Lord at Palani for some time to be provided with at least one meal during their stay.

While there is some confusion about the time and place of the following incident, Nityananda's own words quoted below serve to verify the account. Soon after the young Master left the Pantalayani area, he encountered some cruelly mischievous youths in Cannanore. One of them wrapped a rag soaked in kerosene on the Master's left hand and set it ablaze. Nityananda did not believe in resisting physically, but as his hand was burning like a torch, he transferred the actual sensation of burning to the person who had set the fire. The latter ran about crying in pain and apologizing all at once. Nityananda then extinguished his own burning hand as well as the sensation in the hard of the guilty person. Years later, he told a devotee:

> *Antarjnanis don't go in for miracles. It does not mean ... that if a rag is tied to [his] hand, that it would not burn .... Jnanis also suffer from pain like all others, but they have the capacity to keep their minds completely detached from the nerve centers. Hence they might re- member the pain once or twice in a day.*

Following this largely unrecorded period of travel, the young Nityananda began to appear regularly in the South Kanara district Again, the stories that have survived are episodic and often isolated; a clear chronology is not possible. However, there is agreement that Nityananda, now in his late teens or early twenties, spent several years traveling in the South Kanara area. He sometimes wore a loincloth, sometimes was nude, and lived a life of great simplicity. His home was in the rocks, caves, and forests. It was a familiar sight to see him perched on some tree top, standing stiff. In the early days it became a regular feature to find him on the top of the tree in front of the local Mahakali temple at Kaup. Later he was seen in every part of South Kanara including Mangalore.

Crowds often gathered below the tree on which he stood, crowds that were mixed without regard for caste or creed. After a time, the Master would shower them with leaves; these leaves were greatly prized as medicine. One day a man who had lost his sight stood among the crowd beneath the tree. The others in the crowd eagerly picked up the leaves dropped by Nityananda and went home. Soon only the blind man was left. He continued pleading with the Master to restore his sight, explaining that as it was, he was not able to earn a living and so was a burden to his family. After a considerable time, Nityananda came to him and rubbed the man's eyes with leaves from the tree. No words were spoken, and no change was immediately apparent. However, on arising the next morning, the man was able to see and his sight remained restored.

In Manjeshwar also Nityananda is remembered. In one instance, a man was concerned about his mother who was severely ill with a lump in her calf, accompanied by acute pain and immobility. Medicines offered no relief, so with his mother's permission the man went to Nityananda and asked for help. The Master did not throw down any leaves but only said, *"This one knows and is there."* The son did not understand; he went home and returned with his mother in a carriage. However, when they returned, the Master was gone. Although they searched for him, he was not to be found, so they drove back home. As soon as they entered the house, they heard footsteps on the stairs. To their complete astonishment, it was Nityananda descending from the attic. He massaged the woman's injured leg for a few minutes, then departed wordlessly. The mother recovered and the trouble did not recur.

In this way Nityananda's fame as a healer spread far and wide in South Kanara. Once a widow took her congenitally blind six year old daughter to the Master and pleaded for her eyesight to be restored. Nityananda said, *"But the child has never seen light from its birth. Why are you insisting?"* She nevertheless continued to plead. Nityananda then said, *"Let the child ask what it wants."* The mother told the child to ask for whatever she wanted, and the child said, "I would like to see my mother once." The Master made no response, and after a little time, he asked them to leave. It was the mother's custom to bathe the child first, then put her in a chair and go for her own bath. On this day as she came out of the bath, the little girl leapt up and ran to her, shouting that she could see. But her joy lasted only a few minutes; her blindness returned. Perhaps the Master did not wish to interfere with the irrevocable destiny of the child; perhaps any relief provided now would have interfered with karmic law. However, since the mother was pleading, it appears he left it to the inner voice of the child to say what it wanted and it came out spontaneously that she wanted to see the mother once. This wish was granted.

The following incident occurred in a village in South Kanara; while it is believed to be Panambur, the exact place is not known. It was a bright morning; the busy road was flanked by coconut trees and fields being worked by farmers. A young woman was coming toward the youthful Master, who as usual was walking at his faster-than-wind pace. Suddenly he stopped the woman and squeezed her breasts for a few seconds. Although the woman did not resist, the people on the road rushed towards them. Perhaps they would not have harmed him (some of them had already heard of a young dark person who was healing and feeding the poor), but they were outraged nevertheless. However, Nityananda had already withdrawn by the time the crowd drew near. As he continued walking, he shouted to them not to get excited and that this time the child would not die. He said no more. The woman confirmed that her three previous children had all died at the first breast feeding. She delivered a few days later; this child survived. A delegation from the area went in search of the Master to thank him, and that is how the story came to be spread.

In this case, the Master's unconventional behavior became understandable when more facts about the woman's previous pregnancies and the outcome of the current one were known. Often, however, strange incidents were not so easily understandable. For instance, during this period prior to 1920, the Master would sometimes stand unobtrusively behind some trees in the early hours while it was still dark, and as any cow passed that way, would catch its dropping before it fell on the ground and swallow it. Among the people who noticed this, none had either the courage to ask, or the understanding to comprehend, what it was all about.

Nityananda's own words are eloquent on this subject of the motives of spiritual masters. His words follow a brief description of another unconventional incident, that of walking across the river Pavanje at full flood. The Master wanted to go to the other side, but since it was the monsoon season and the river was in flood, the boatman refused perhaps because he did not wish to risk it for one person. Without a second thought, the Master then simply walked across.

When asked in 1953 to explain the meaning of this, he said:

> It is true that the Pavanje River was in flood at the time this one walked across, and that the boatman would not venture out. But it was not done with any motivation. It happened automatically—during the mood of the moment. But what is the use of all that? It only meant depriving the boatman of his half anna. One must live in the world like common men.... Once one is established in infinite consciousness, one becomes silent and though knowing everything, goes about as if he does not know anything. Though he might be doing a lot of things in several places, to all outward appearance he will remain as if he does nothing. He will always remain as if

*he is a witness to everything that goes on, like a spectator at
a cinema show, and is not affected by the pleasant or the unpleasant. To be able to forget everything and be aloof, that
alone is the highest state to be in.*

Similarly, Nityananda was indifferent to conventions of clothing and
often went about nude in the early days. Some of the locals objected
and in due course reported the matter. Nityananda was taken to a local
Magistrate with a crowd following him. When asked why he would not
wear a loincloth, he reportedly replied, *"To cover which with what?"*
The Magistrate ordered the police to tie a loincloth. The order was duly
followed, but each time the string was tied around his hips, it slipped
down no matter how tightly it was tied. Devotees suggested sending for
a tailor in the neighborhood who was a devotee of the Master. The
tailor-devotee pleaded with Nityananda to allow the langoti he was
tying to stay in place. It remained, and Nityananda was clothed with a
loincloth, as he would be until his passing.

In Kanhangad in those early years (circa 1915) Nityananda spent
most of his time on the beach. He would lie from morning till evening
on the sands, gazing at the sun. A devotee who as a little boy often accompanied his father to Kanhangad told me how impossible it was to
approach the Master in the afternoons, owing to the burning sands.
Sometimes he would be found on the rock where his first temple (constructed in 1963) now stands. He would lie there on the rock from
morning till evening; one person told me that he had gone all the way
from North Kanara to Kanhangad to see him but could not go anywhere near him the whole day owing to the burning rock.

Discovery in Udipi

In 1918, Udipi was still quite small, but was nevertheless a well-
known center of pilgrimage. Pilgrims came to the Krishna temple, the
birthplace of the third great *Acharya,* Madhvacharya, the ancient
Ananteshwar temple, and the wooded area called Ajjara Kadu (mean-

ing grandfathers' wood). Two friends [10] walked together here each evening and would end their walk by going around the two temples. One evening while passing the Krishna temple, the friends were attracted by the young, lean, bright looking Nityananda standing among the sanyasis in the outer corridors of the Krishna temple. The moment Nityananda saw them, he turned towards the wall, declining to be met or recognized. This only intrigued the gentlemen and they agreed that he was definitely an uncommon sadhu. A few days later, they came upon Nityananda standing in one of the entrances of the temple. He was seized by a bout of prolonged laughter. He would neither talk nor recognize them but continued laughing. Mr. Bhat, one of the two gentlemen, told me that it was not common laughter because it appeared to be spontaneously exuding from the innermost depths of his being.

One afternoon a few weeks later they met him again in the outer porches of the ancient Ananteshwar temple. There was no one else present; he was seated alone. The doctor immediately caught hold of both his hands and addressing him in Hindi, Kanarese, and English in quick succession, inquired who he was and where he came from. The Master gave the impression that he had been observing silence for a long period, as it obviously required effort for him to speak. After a struggle he responded in fluent English, Hindi, and Konkani (their own local language).

He also repeated, *"nityananda, nityananda."* The doctor and Mr Bhat knew that this was not a name, but that the young master was referring to his blissful state. It is for this reason that most devotees of the South Kanara days call him "Sadhu" or "Swami."

Both the doctor and Mr. Bhat were greatly enthused and the latter invited him to his house for a meal, saying that he had performed his father's anniversary ceremony that morning. To their great delight, the Master readily accepted the invitation. He ate from a plantain leaf with his own hands and threw away the leaf himself. This was the first and last time that the young Master ate with his own hands during his sojourn in South Kanara. After this, he ate only if and when fed by devotees. He would not even ask for water; devotees would from time to

---

[10]The late Dr. R. Kombarbail and the late Mr. K. Shivanna Bhat. I contacted Mr. Bhat in Bombay in 1966 to get a brief version of the circumstances in which the two of them first met Nityananda. Dr. Kombarbail later became a well-known physician in Bombay, and being practically a sanyasi householder, he rarely billed his patients and many times financed the poorer ones—the right type of man to discover a great Master.

time pour some into his mouth, and after a couple of swallows, he would indicate he was satisfied.

Nityananda stayed in Udipi for some time, but he was never in one place for long; he frequently went to Mangalore and Kaup, but everywhere his movements were unpredictable.

It is quite possible that his frequent and apparently erratic movements from place to place had something to do with the mystical magnetic pull of devotees thinking of him, or otherwise undergoing some stress or strain. Mrs. T. Sitabai, who was my main source for the incidents connected with his stay in Udipi, used to say that he would often leave very suddenly without indicating where he was going, and return only after a long period. On one such occasion, he was sitting with the devotees when he suddenly got up at 3:30 P.M. and said that he would return soon. No one knew where he had gone but he did return by about 5:00 P.M. No one asked him where he had been, nor did he indicate the place he visited. A couple of days later, a devotee came from Mangalore and during the conversation said that the Master had been with them two evenings ago for about an hour and a half from 3:30 to 5:00 P.M., when he left saying that some people were waiting for him. Earlier that afternoon, the devotees in Mangalore had assembled and were speaking sincerely of how nice it would be to see the Master again. Within a few minutes, he made his appearance. On this occasion, as on others, no one inquired how he covered the 50-odd miles by road to Mangalore. The incident is narrated not to raise this question, but to show how he could not resist, when remembered longingly by the devout.

A similar incident took place in Mrs. Krishnabai's* house in Mangalore. It was to be Nityananda's first visit to their house, but the moment he arrived, he refused to stay, instead walking towards the north with his usual speed. There was a crowd watching as Mrs. Krishnabai's husband and another friend tried to restrain him. But thin as he was, he was carrying both of these men with ease and had gone at least a quarter mile before he suddenly stopped and agreed to return. Mrs. Krishnabai had been preparing lovingly for the Master's intended visit, since it was to have been his first visit to her home and she was anxious to show him her devotion through her hospitality. As a result, she was very sad that he had gone and was thinking of him intensely.

One of the earliest known devotees. She and her contemporaries, Mrs. Sitabai and Mrs. Muktabai, reappear frequently in these stories.

Nityananda on his way back to Mrs. Krishnabai's house told the two men who had so ineffectively tried to restrain him: *"She stopped me."* The magnetic pull of her feelings was too much to be ignored.

At first, street urchins in Udipi tried to pelt the young Nityananda with stones to keep him away from the Krishna temple, particularly on festive occasions. Each time a stone struck him, it would scintillate. There would be a rush to pick up the marvelous objects, but by the time they reached the ground they were mere stones again. (In Kanhangad, there was an incident of stones falling as sweets.) A few days later a large number of stones were found at the feet of the Krishna statue in the famous shrine. This matter was reported to the elderly Swami in charge of the monastery. He was aware that Nityananda was no ordinary sadhu and had already issued instructions to treat him with respect and consideration. These were emphasized as a result of this incident.

Throughout his life, Nityananda was associated with caring for, and especially feeding, the poor. In South Kanara he was a friend of the beggars, the poor and the low-caste. He was the same in Ganeshpuri and he is the same today. In Mangalore, visiting devotees would leave money, often gold sovereigns, at his feet; he would ask his hostess to collect this money and put it aside. After a few days he would ask how much money there was and then would order a feast for the poor. He would insist on using the best ingredients and would himself join in the serving. This was a regular feature wherever he went. In later years he would only accept invitations if the host was prepared to feed the poor. Even at Ganeshpuri, the feeding of the poor was a frequent and regular feature. Food brought as offering by devotees would be distributed among the local poor children, and special *Bal Bhojan* feasts were often arranged.

A most unusual feature of his feeding the poor was that even if the quantity of food appeared inadequate for the number present, the servers were nonetheless exhorted to serve liberally. In the end there was always enough to go around. Many such instances were narrated to me as having occurred in Ganeshpuri. And whenever the Master himself served, particularly items which were served by the hands (such as *iddlies* cooked in jackfruit leaves as in Mangalore), he would dig in with both of his huge palms, serving in such large quantities that the host would be certain there wouldn't be enough food—yet everyone who came would be satisfied.

Many local people helped the Master organize and pay for these feedings of the poor, often to the chagrin of well-placed husbands or parents who considered the Master a young eccentric. Among those who sought his company in Udipi was a young schoolboy, the only son of a well-placed local landlord, who would occasionally bring money from his father. The Master put this money into the collections for feeding the poor. The father, convinced that Nityananda was merely an eccentric from whose influence his son needed protection, apparently decided that the surest way to save his son was to remove Nityananda entirely. He felt certain that no one would be seriously concerned about his disappearance or an accidental mishap. Nor was it so very unusual in those days for people of means to arrange for such disposals in the villages.

In this case, it seemed reasonable to assume that the Master's disappearance would not give immediate cause for alarm, since such disappearances were part of his normal behavior. The landlord accordingly hired two assassins. One afternoon the Master was sitting with a large number of devotees on a veranda when he suddenly leapt up smiling, and disappeared down the lane. Although the devotees were used to such sudden departures, on this occasion they ran after him. By the time they reached him, he was being held tightly by one person and was about to be stabbed by another. The devotees overpowered both attackers and wrested the knife from the attempted assassin. Their shouts attracted several policemen; there was great confusion. As the excitement began to die down and the noise subsided, the assassin could be heard pleading for help. He shouted that they could do whatever they liked with him, only please restore his hand, which was in great pain. It was only then noticed that his hand was frozen in the raised position. Although several people tried, it was no use; his arm would not come down. The young Master then approached the man and touched his arm. The would-be assassin was immediately relieved from the excruciating pain he was suffering, and he regained the use of his arm. Both assailants were taken to the police station and locked up after appropriate charges were lodged.

Nityananda protested and urged that they be released, but no one would listen to him. He thereupon took up a vigil outside the jail, saying that he would not move till the men were released. He remained there for three days without food or water, whether it was sun or shade, day or night. Meanwhile devotees negotiated with the officials, asking that the two men be released for the sake of the Master and the stand he was taking. It took some effort but ultimately the two men were set free. As a result, not only did the would-be assassins become devotees of the Master, but the local officials were also chastened and began to develop a sneaking regard for the fiber of this "eccentric sadhu."

Late one evening during the early Udipi days, a devotee was told by the women of his household that the young Master was running a high temperature but that he was lying on the floor of the cattle-shed, in the midst of the cattle and their offal. He refused to leave. saying, *"The medicine is here."* He repeated the same thing to all who went to plead with him. No one could guess his meaning. Finally, after much pleading by his host, he agreed to leave the shed and sleep on the veranda.

The devotee went to the only chemist in Udipi and returned with a large bottle of reddish-brown mixture for the Master's fever. Nityananda took the bottle, shook it, and handed it back, asking *"What have you brought? Is this a mixture? See properly."* When the cork was removed, the devotee found to his consternation that the liquid smelled very much like cow's urine, and the color also had changed. The Master laughed, saying it was no better than the stuff he could have gotten in the cattle-shed.

That night at about 8 P.M. the Master suddenly began drinking rain water from the drum in front of the house. It was the period of the South-West monsoon, and during this period it was customary to keep a large drum below the eaves to collect rain water. The drum was nearly full that evening. Witnesses could not believe he could drink all that water. When he returned to the house, he said, *"Where is the fever? It's all gone."* It had in fact gone.

The Master utilized unconventional remedies for the ills of others as well. An Udipi devotee's wife had been delivered of a child six days before. In those days, a special ceremony was performed on the sixth day, as it was believed that the goddess of destiny was going to write the child's future on the evening of that day. That night the Master entered the room of the mother and child, swallowed the dried remnant of the child's umbilical cord, and walked out. When asked by shocked devotees why he had done this, he replied that many children of this family had passed away in infancy but this one would live.

During this time in Udipi the Master would sometimes indicate who would be visiting during the day by a one-man acting show. One morning, he slung an empty cloth marketing bag over his left shoulder, bending a little as if it were heavy. In his right hand he mimed carrying something lighter, as he paced up and down the room. The people in the house did not understand what he was trying to say. Suddenly he rushed out towards a neighbor's house, followed by the devotees. In the street, they saw a man walking up and down apparently in search of someone. He was carrying a heavy bag slung over his left shoulder, bending a little as a result, and holding a *kamandalu* (container that sanyasis carry for water) in his right hand. The Master sat on the first step of the neighbor's veranda and the stranger stopped in front of him; they gazed wordlessly at one another for a very long period. Finally the Master stood and the stranger walked away. No words had been exchanged.

During the next several days, the visitor remained in Udipi. Various devotees questioned him about this unusual encounter. The visitor replied that he was a Krishna devotee from Uttar Pradesh. While in Mathura, he had a vision conveying to him that Krishna was present in living form in Udipi. From the vision, he received a rough idea of the area and he felt he was vibrationally directed to this place. However, having come this far, he was not sure of the exact house and that was why he had been walking up and down when the Master appeared. He added, "There was no need to talk because as soon as I saw him I knew what I was looking for. I had Krishna darshan and am going back tomorrow blissfully happy with the vision vouchsafed to me this morning."

Mrs. Sitabai wistfully recalled one of her own early interactions with the young Master at Udipi. One day the Master picked up a coconut and offered it to the young married woman. It is a rare opportunity to receive a coconut from a holy person, and is generally held to be an auspicious symbol. A married woman would traditionally extend a portion of her sari with both hands to receive it as a special benediction to to keep widowhood away from her. But she was filled with doubts. She thought about her high-caste birth, and whether it would be correct for her to accept anything like this from the casteless Nityananda. The Master waited for several minutes but as she would not accept the offering, he threw it away, perhaps regretting that fate was too powerful for her. Three months later she was widowed. Recently she wondered if perhaps she would have been spared youthful widowhood if her faith in the Master had been stronger.

The following extraordinary incident occurred in Mangalore at Mrs. Krishnabai's house some time in the very early twenties when the Master was a frequent visitor. As indicated earlier, with the exception of the meal he took on the day of his discovery in the Ananteshwar temple at Udipi, he had to be fed throughout the next few years in South Kanara. That applied to drinking water as well; his eating habits were as erratic as his movements. He would often appear unexpectedly at Mrs. Krishnabai's home and ask indirectly if there was anything there. Often if the family had already had their dinner, there would be only a little leftover rice stored in water, near the dishes stacked for washing by the servant in the morning. Nityananda would reply that this would do, and a few morsels of that put in his mouth would satisfy him. There was no knowing when or what he would eat.

Also important to this story is a sketch of the compound containing the Krishnabai residence. Attached to their big house were four or five others which were rented. In those days the dry lavatories were situated in a line at the end of the large compound, to be used by all the residents of the building. The night-soil was collected every morning, and loaded on carts for disposal as arranged by the local municipal authorities.

One morning the occupants of the four or five houses in the compound were horrified to see the Master sitting near the lavatories, with large heaps of night-soil in front of him. He must have gotten up very early, collected the matter with his own hands, and formed the heaps behind which he was sitting. In addition, he had covered himself with it from head to foot; face, lips, and all. He held an improvised bamboo weighing balance in his hand, and each time a person passed him on the way to the lavatories, he said, *"Bombay halwa—very tasty—want to eat? Can weigh and give you some."* With that he would raise the balance as if to weigh out the quantity asked for. Everyone felt embarrassed, but he sat there the whole day. In the afternoon, he slept in the midst of those heaps. When Mrs. Krishnabai went to him in the afternoon, he told her, *"You feed me, don't you? But would you also feed me with the stuff kept here?"* She also turned back.

The Master spent the whole day by the heaps he had made. In the evening Mrs. Krishnabai was afraid that he would drop in without washing. Devotees had already assembled. Two of them waited at the entrances to ensure that the Master did not bring the dirt inside. At about seven in the evening, he came and stood at the rear entrance. In those days, he could be prevailed upon at least in some matters; the two devotees took him to the baths for a thorough scrubbing and wash. Sitting amidst the devotees later, he held out his palm and asked whether they would like to smell it: *"Fine Paris perfume,"* he said. He neither explained nor did others inquire about the meaning of the day's event.

The next morning all the neighbors were lined up in front of the Master asking his pardon. Drawing one of them aside, Mrs. Krishnabai inquired what had happened for them to seek a pardon. The neighbor said "There was general talk among us the other day about Nityananda taking food only if fed. Some of us sarcastically asked whether he would eat if he were fed night-soil. We now see that we had misjudged him; he has shown us that even that can be eaten by a person of his stature. Hence we are seeking his pardon."

Mangalore: Rail Travel

The decade before Nityananda settled at Ganeshpuri (1923-1933) was punctuated with much travel, particularly on the railroad. He often went to Mangalore and at times lived in the railroad boxcars after they were shunted aside at terminal stations. He was fond of the railway; even his Kanhangad Ashram is next to the railway track. He often traveled in the engine car with the driver, where he was especially welcome after some of the incidents outlined below. In Mangalore, the news that he could be found at the station in one of the boxcars soon reached the devotees, who would go there to have his darshan. How the news of his arrival spread about so quickly is not known.

The following incident took place on one such occasion. Increasing restrictions concerning visiting the Master were placed on Mrs. Krishnabai during his later years in Mangalore. On this occasion, like all other devotees she heard that he was in Mangalore and that he was staying in one of the cars in the yard, so she went hurriedly, had darshan and returned.

That evening a relative who was a sanyasi arrived for a short stay. Hearing of the Master's presence in town, he went to see him the next evening, and took Mrs. Krishnabai with him. As she was going with her relative, apparently there were no restrictions. They had darshan and as they were stepping down from the boxcar, Mrs. Krishnabai told the Master, "When I came here yesterday for a hurried visit, I never imagined that I would be coming today and for a longer period as well." The Master replied, *"Who are you to decide?"*

There are numerous incidents connected with the railroad during this period of frequent travel between Mangalore and Kanhangad. One relates to his being asked to leave the train at Manjeshwar because he had not shown a ticket. A new railroad official forcibly removed him from the train. Nityananda surrendered to the rough handling, and sat on a bench at the station. When it was time for the train to depart, it would not move. After a few minutes some of the passengers approached the official saying that Nityananda was not an ordinary sanyasi and should not be so harshly treated. Some devotees then took Nityananda on board and the train started at once. When it reached Kanhangad, it continued past the station, actually stopping where his Ashram is now situated. When Nityananda descended, he was wearing a garland made of hundreds of tickets (of all three or four classes in vogue then). He handed the garland to the same official, asking him to take the one he wanted. The man was ashamed of the rough treatment he had meted out, and confessed that he was new to the line but this would not happen again. Nityananda nodded, then jumped the small ditch and strode off toward the jungle. Again the train would not move, and again devotees ran to the Master for help. He retraced his steps, gently slapped the engine and asked it to move. It did so, going in reverse back to the station it had bypassed earlier.

Perhaps because of incidents such as these Nityananda had free run of these trains, and he was always welcome in the engine car. The drivers would blow a saluting whistle as they passed his Ashram; even today some drivers do this. In the late twenties, whenever he traveled, his ticket was found sewn on the string which tied his loin cloth. It used to have a punched hole as well.

Swami Chidananda of Rishikesh recalled an incident from his childhood. He had been traveling south by train from Mangalore. At one of the way-side stations he heard a joyous uproar. Peering out of the window, he saw the reed thin Nityananda throwing biscuits and sweets from a vendor's tray over the station railing to a small crowd of delighted children scrambling to retrieve them outside. He then pulled a currency note from his loincloth for the vendor, who appeared pleased. As the departing whistle blew, Nityananda walked to the engine car and climbed up.

His association with the railway recalls two other incidents. One was often witnessed in the streets of Udipi. He would at times be seen in the middle of the road (there was hardly any motor traffic in those days), catching the dropping from a cow before it fell to the ground, putting it on his head, and then whistling just like a railway engine and chugging away, as children often do.

And it was to the railroad that he turned in his last speech for symbols and illustrations. Only twelve days before his mahasamadhi, on Guru Purnima day (July 27, 1961), he spoke to his assembled devotees at some length, using the example of the energy needed to pull a train up an incline and of the necessity of staying firmly on the rails. Perhaps his earlier pranks of sitting in the engine car were but a simple way of announcing that an engine was available if the cars were ready.

This period of constant travel from Mangalore to Kanhangad to Udipi to Akroli and so on forced the Master's devotees to be very alert as well as very flexible; it was never known with certainty when and where he would be available for darshan. At times he would appear almost as if by magic and cause all plans to change. The following incident involves some devotees from Udipi along with a trio of non-human "devotees." The Udipi devotees had decided to go visiting since they understood that Nityananda had gone to Mangalore. Six or seven of them set out together; they had to pass through a wooded area. As they approached this area, they were surprised to see Nityananda sitting under a tree some distance away. The devotees immediately gave up the idea of social calling and decided to spend the evening there. Nityananda shouted to them not to come any nearer as there were cobras around. They sat down where they were, at least 15 or 20 feet away. They could hear Nityananda speaking, and peered into the gloom to see the other person, but no one could be seen. As their eyes adjusted to the light, they saw a little cobra sitting near him—

he was talking to it in Konkani. The cobra seemed to be nodding but it was impossible to know whether it had anything to do with what was being spoken to it. Nor could they hear the Master's words owing to the distance, except for one sentence which carried clearly: *"Are the three of you comfortable inside?"* From this they inferred there were two other cobras inside the hole. Shortly afterwards, he patted the little cobra on the hood and it also disappeared.

Indeed, the Master's behavior was often difficult to interpret. Sometimes it appeared that some minor trouble was created or forced upon one, while later reflection would indicate that perhaps some more serious trouble had thus been averted. Sincere devotees will appreciate this statement from their own personal experience. Such a situation was related by a Mangalore devotee. As a young man, the Master often visited her home. Once, when her married daughter was present, the boyish Master said to the daughter, *"She is this one's mother; your mother is here* [indicating himself]." In those days the hearths were on the ground, either made of mud or ready-made of tile. Firewood was used in the main opening. One evening the Master walked into the devotee's kitchen as she was cooking, pulled out a burning piece of firewood, hit her on the head with it, and quickly disappeared. Her children were greatly offended and angrily demanded retaliation but the mother advised patience. No explanation was sought or provided for this outrage. A year later an expert astrologer from Kerala was engaged to cast the family horoscopes. He was greatly astonished to find the lady of the house alive. He said that according to the stars, she would have died a year ago or at least been so seriously ill that full recovery was not indicated. It was then that the family realized that the blow given that evening had resulted in some adjustment.

In the early twenties, Mrs. Lakshmibai was a young widow working as a domestic for Tulsiamma, a well-known devotee of the Master. The young widow was also devoted to him. Late one evening, she was told to get the meal ready soon, as her employer and another devotee were leaving to bring the Master back for dinner. Mrs. Lakshmibai had always nursed an intense desire to feed the Master. Seeing him being fed by other devotees, she hoped for a chance to render this service, but owing to her status and her shyness, she was not bold enough to do it on her own. This evening she asked to accompany her employer in the hope that even if the Master did not come to their home, she might volunteer to feed him wherever he was. However she was told that she had better do the cooking, so that if the Master came he could be readily offered some food. So saying, Tulsiamma and her friend left.

Mrs. Lakshmibai prepared the meal and when everything was ready, went into the compound of the house to cut some plantain leaves to use for serving. It was quite dark, and the plantain trees were some distance away. She was still feeling hurt about not being offered a chance to visit the Master that evening, and was not at all sure that she would be allowed to feed him. Her musing was interrupted by the rustle of plantain leaves as she was about to cut one of them. To her surprise and awe, Nityananda was standing there. Asking, *"Is the food ready?"*, he proceeded into the house. Mrs. Lakshmibai was overjoyed; with the one leaf she had just cut, she ran inside, washed her hands and started feeding the Master. Just as she finished, Tulsiamma arrived at the gate, saying, "We could not find him." To their pleasant surprise they found the Master there enjoying his dinner.

Mr. Appayya Alva was a well known figure in the social circles of South Kanara. He was a successful landlord, but perhaps was even better known as a powerful *mantravadi*, able to materialize objects. He was welcome in the best homes and was treated with respect, although he also occasioned some fear because of his reputed powers over astral agencies. At marriage ceremonies, if the family was known to him, Mr. Alva might produce out-of-season fruits or flowers by the bundle, with a mere movement of his hands. Of course, it later transpired that whenever he materialized these things, there was a simultaneous outcry elsewhere, where the articles had suddenly disappeared. This was particularly the experience of the flower-maids in the Car Street flower market in Mangalore. They would suddenly wail, "Oh! My flowers have gone!" Apparently, many people suffered that way. Similarly he would produce exotic cigarettes in tins for friends if they asked for them.

Once in the very early twenties, a music concert had been arranged in the house of a well-to-do person in Mangalore with a musician from Bangalore. Mr. Alva happened to be in town and intended to attend the concert, but was unfortunately stopped at the gate by someone who did not know him. Mr. Alva took umbrage at not being recognized or admitted and reportedly said that he would like to see how the program would go on. It did not, because the singer simply could not sing.

That was Mr. Alva. He had heard about Nityananda and the large number of devotees and admirers that were following him. On this day in May, 1923, Mr. M.A.K. Rao, a major landlord in Manjeshwar, was celebrating his niece's wedding. The family insisted that Nityananda sit on a chair while the couple garlanded him and received his blessings. Just then Mr. Alva walked in.

Mr. Alva spoke disparagingly of the young Master, and expressed his surprise at the gullibility of the family in honoring him as if he were a divine being. He said that if the Master were genuine, then he would accept a challenge from Mr. Alva. The hosts tried to dissuade Mr. Alva from such blasphemous demonstrations, but he would not listen. He said he was going to see whether Nityananda was a genuine yogi or whether all the tales growing around him were merely made up by interested parties. He then rolled a tobacco leaf with his hands for some time, apparently using a mantra, and forced it into the Master's mouth. As will be recalled, the Master never ate anything on his own, and anything that was put into his mouth was eaten. The Master chewed and ate the leaf as if it were any morsel of food given by a loving devotee. The Master perspired a little after swallowing the tobacco leaf, but nothing else happened. On the other hand, in the wedding hall, Mr. Alva suddenly became so dizzy that he could not stand; he sank to the ground. Attempts to make him comfortable failed; he continued to feel worse and asked to be taken to a friend's home. He was taken there, but his condition continued to decline. The next morning he was moved to the Government Wenlock Hospital in Mangalore, where he passed away on the third day after the incident.

When the Master was asked about this incident many years later in 1953, he said,

It is not correct to say that Appayya Alva died immediately after he administered the tobacco leaf to this one. Mr. Rao was keen that this one should be garlanded first by the

couple to be married and that afterwards the actual wedding ceremony should take place. So someone came to take this one from the neighboring hill [known as Bungalow Hill]. Mr. Alva also attended. He was a big mantravadi and used to do many things for many people with his mantrasiddhi. Normally people were afraid of him. He was also conscious that he was a very big mantravadi. When this one was brought to the marriage hall, made to sit on a chair and garlanded, he was upset that while no such honor was being shown to him, why it should have been shown to an ordinary sadhu like this one.

The Master deprecated any effort to establish a connection between the administration of the tobacco leaf and Mr. Alva's demise, as seen in the quote above. He stated that Alva's considerable mantric powers had been misused, causing much suffering to the poor and the weak, and the divine forces had obviously decided to cry a halt to the abuse of such supernatural powers. The tobacco leaf came only as a *nimithya* (immediate nominal cause). He then added that Mr. Alva started repenting that he had made a mistake and wondering whether his trouble was due to the tobacco leaf given to the sanyasi (i.e. Nityananda). Alva requested that he might be taken to the Master or the sanyasi brought to him. Perhaps the family was too proud to do this; however, there is no doubt that the Master helped Mr. Alva in his last moments.

Also in 1923, during the height of the monsoon, Nityananda was walking through the market place in Bantwal. Looking back, it is possible that he went there to see whether God would provide a chance to save the place from the impending disaster. As it was raining heavily, he took shelter in one of the shops, standing in the corner where servants and coolies normally sat when they were not otherwise employed. The owners ordered him out, laughing and taunting him with jeering questions about his reputed immunity from the elements, since they had recognized him as Nityananda. The Master's name was becoming well known in the district, and adulation and skepticism existed side by side. These shopkeepers had heard of the recent incident involving Mr. Alva, and chose to adopt an aggressive attitude to show that they were not afraid. Nityananda pleaded with them, saying that since it was raining very hard, they might allow him to stand in a corner. They then started splashing water on him and having a good laugh. Appearing very sad, the Master walked away saying, *"It would appear that God has decided that only mother Ganga shall wash the sins of this place."* The shopkeepers who heard him mockingly retorted,"Oh! let her come, we would greet her and not go home. We will sit here and wash ourselves by just bending and filling our mugs."

Even as they spoke the noise and rumble of the swollen river grew and the Netravati started rolling in. It was one of the worst floods in South Kanara, and Bantwal was laid waste. One of the spans of the Ullal railway bridge was also badly damaged and train service was disorganized for a few months. It is believed that Nityananda saved many poor people, by swimming in the swirling waters. There was a suggestion that the floods came because of the insults heaped on Nityananda, but it was not so; rather he was perhaps prevented from being able to be more helpful in reducing the suffering already decided upon by the Divine Force.

The most extraordinary incident that occurred during his sojourn in Mangalore related to what may be termed his first mahasamadhi. It was some time between 1922-23, and took place in the house of a devotee in an area known as Falnir in Mangalore. Various devotees were seated in front of Nityananda for a meditational exercise that evening. It was about sunset when they were suddenly disturbed by a blinding flash of light on the wall behind the Master. When they opened their eyes, they found Nityananda on his haunches in a sort of hero-lotus posture (*veera-padmasana*) with his eyes closed; there was no movement. Soon the lamps were lit. Memory of the blinding flash combined with the stiffness of the Master's limbs in the pose made them think that perhaps *rigor mortis* had already set in. No one dared to touch him or send for a doctor, but they conducted other tests for breath, such as holding a piece of cotton and then a mirror in front of his nose. No breath could be detected; they shook their heads in despair.

They still did not touch him but sent word of his mahasamadhi to all the devotees, inviting them to come and have the last darshan. After spending a little time, most of the devotees returned to their homes sad and disappointed, as they had entertained high hopes and expectations of the youthful master. Now they felt a sudden void in their lives and a sense of confusion and insecurity. Others believed that he would return and there were also those who had not yet had their faith firmly established who thought that perhaps he had overdone some breathing exercise to his detriment.

A few devotees remained with the host, maintaining a vigil throughout the night and the next day. Late the next afternoon, Nityananda suddenly showed signs of slight movement. He seemed to stretch his limbs and was immediately helped to a bed. He had a strange look about him and did not recognize any one for quite some time. After repeated questions from those nearby, he replied casually but in a rather disjointed manner. He said he had gone for good, but *"the time was not yet,"* and the five divine personalities who met him persuaded him to return. He never touched on this subject again, and if questioned either changed the subject or said that it was nothing. I owe this narrative to Mrs. Krishnabai who was one of the devotees that visited him both during and after the incident.

Kanhangad: The Rock Ashram

Following this time of travel centered on Mangalore and before the Master's final departure from South Kanara, he began to spend long periods in Kanhangad, beginning in 1925. At first he used the area known as Guruvana as his base. Just a few miles from the Rock Ashram, this jungle area is the site of the second temple dedicated to Nityananda (in 1966). As recorded earlier, it is believed without any possibility of verification that he was found outside this jungle as a discarded infant. There is evidence indicating that he spent some time in a cave in this area which has since been blocked up. It is believed that a skeleton seated in the lotus posture and surrounded by some pots and other personal articles was found in this jungle cave. Nityananda is thought to have disposed of these in a manner not known to others. This was narrated to me by an elderly lady from Kerala, who used to feed Nityananda in the Guruvana period. It is further believed that at the end of the cave, which is now blocked, there was an entrance to a hall that would seat several hundred. Nityananda often said that beyond the hill in Guruvana there were many saints in samadhi. At one time some people believed that the Master had been associated with this jungle in his previous incarnation and that the skeleton was either his own or that of someone he knew.

It was here that Nityananda struck a rock and brought out spring water, which has been flowing ever since. When the temple was constructed in 1966 by Mr. B.H. Mehta, a spout was constructed for the water to flow. It is called Papanashini Ganga. Nearby, Nityananda created eight stone balls thought to represent eight siddhis, and a spring water tank.

For many years this area was tended by Swami Janananda who converted the jungle into a spiritual paradise. He rebuilt the tank as a well, constructed a road leading to the temple, and placed eight stone *linga*-like structures in the place of the stone balls said to have been created by Nityananda to represent the *ashtasiddhis*. There is also a small shrine for Malbir, the protecting spirit of the area.

It is not known exactly when the Master began construction work in the Kanhangad fort area, but it was about 1927. He first constructed a road which still stands, running from the Travelers' Bungalow up to the rock temple and Ashram. Then he began clearing the jungle within the dilapidated fort. Historically, the fort had been held by a long line of chieftains; at one time it was in the hands of the Tulu dynasty ruling the area from Mangalore to Kanhangad. When Nityananda started clearing the jungle, he used to say that one day government offices would be situated there. This has happened. He was often questioned by the local authorities about his purpose in clearing the area and with whose permission he was doing so. As stated above, he would merely say that some day their offices would be there; he was clearing the jungle for them.

After clearing the fort area, Nityananda turned his attention to the rock, where the first temple erected for him in 1963 now stands. He wished to have "sunrise—sunset" caves hewn from the rock. There were no engineers or blueprints; all directions down to the most minute details were provided by the Master. The task was formidable; it was a matter of virtually scooping out the caves by hand. Within two to three years, about 40 caves were dug. They were properly cemented and plastered inside and out. There were six entrances, three of them facing the east and three facing the west. As a result, there was continuous light throughout the aisles, from sunrise to sunset. Most of the caves were large enough for one to sit and rest. There was also a well dug inside the caves. This was closed later, after the Master issued instructions from Ganeshpuri. Another well dug just outside the rock remains the main source of water for the Ashram today.

Local laborers were hired for this construction and clearing of the caves. While this was not at all unusual, Swami Janananda recalled that the manner in which the Master paid the workers at the end of the day was peculiar. Most of the time, the man in charge of the workmen was told to collect the amount from under a tree, where the exact change would be lying. At other times, the workers would file past the Master as he sat nearby. As he opened and closed his empty fist, the correct wages would fall into the hand of each worker.

After a time, the local authorities began to take more serious notice of the Master's activities. When a delegation arrived one day to question him about the source of the workers' wage money, Nityananda took them to the waterlogged field next to the rock, took a deep dive and came out with a bagful of notes. He told the astonished officials that there was a crocodile inside, which had any amount of money and if they so wished they could also try or else he would get the crocodile and they could tackle it.

Angry at being so defied by a mere sanyasi in a loincloth, the local authorities reported to the Collector of South Kanara that a sanyasi was making unauthorized constructions and moreover was paying his workers with money from unknown, mysterious sources. The English Collector, Mr. Gawne, had been told by his subordinates about the remarkable activities of Nityananda during his sojourn in Mangalore. Feeling rather curious, Gawne went to Kanhangad himself. He rode on horseback from the railway station, and was accompanied by his dog. As he rode down the road constructed by Nityananda, he halted near the rock and started looking for the Master, who was not visible. Actually Nityananda was sitting in the cave just below the ruins of the old fort on the southern side almost facing the rock. The dog soon traced him and started barking outside the cave. When Nityananda came out, the Collector asked him why and for whom he was doing all this. Nityananda replied in English, *"Not for this one; if you want you may have it."* As soon as these words were uttered, there was a sudden change in Gawne; he called the local authorities aside and told them that Nityananda should not be disturbed, and that he should have the free run of the place to do what he liked. As for the money, he was not bothered, provided they had no complaint from any one about being swindled or otherwise having their monies missing. There was a surprise waiting for Mr. Gawne and the local officials. As he was riding back, when he neared the Travelers' Bungalow, he saw a large board erected on which was painted "Gawne Road." It had not been there minutes before, when he was riding down to the rock. For several years after this incident, this road was known as Gawne Road

While the work was in progress inside the rock, the Master often worked on the outside. The structures resembling steps and lingas were done by his own hand. After seeing the caves in 1945, I asked the Master at Ganeshpuri what it all meant. He cryptically told me that it represented the brain, and that just like the brain, it also had six inlets. The step-like structures may represent layers of the brain. It is not clear what the linga-like structures represent.

Swami Janananda narrated the following incident from the time of the cave construction. It was a cloudy day during the monsoon period and the Master was lying on the rock. He was approached by a blustering man who demanded that if Nityananda was such a great man, then let God be revealed to him. Nityananda did not respond to his request; he simply asked to be left alone, but this only made the man more aggressive. Nityananda then just grabbed his umbrella and aimed its point at the man's toe. Perhaps as the dormant energy in the man was rendered kinetic and hit the *Brahmarandra* (literally, the opening to God in the head), the man screamed and fainted. When he revived, he went to the government hospital for external treatment. The doctor in charge came to the rock to see the Master; he reported to the police that Nityananda appeared insane and possibly dangerous. The police promptly took Nityananda to the station and brought him before the Magistrate. When Nityananda declared that nothing had been done by him (by 'this one' as he would have said), the Magistrate asked whether he had any witnesses. The Master pointed to the four pillars of the hall and said that they were his witnesses. Thinking he really was out of his mind, the Magistrate ordered Nityananda locked up.

After some time, the Master told the duty constable that he wanted to urinate. He was given a receptacle, but in moments it was filled and overflowing. Another was brought, but with the same result. A clay water pot was offered next, but when this too began to overflow, the police had to consider that this was an extraordinary individual as reported. The duty policemen went to the Magistrate and suggested that it would do no good for them to keep him in restraint and that he might as well be permitted to go wherever he wanted. The Magistrate agreed and thus the Master returned to the rock after just a few hours, still in time to disburse wages that evening.

On the other hand, when the government doctor who had declared the Master insane returned to his home for lunch he was shocked to find his wife dancing away without any clothes. She was obviously in a temporary state of insanity. The doctor rushed to the police station and upon learning that Nityananda had been released, came to the rock and sought his benediction for the hasty diagnosis. The Master waved him away and all returned to normal.

During those days, Swami Janananda noted other unusual occurrences around the Master. On many occasions he would emerge from the water tank after his morning bath without being wet. When he came inside, even his loincloth would be completely dry. Similarly, Swami Janananda noticed that the Master would be quite dry even after coming through rain.

This incident from these early days in Kanhangad outside the Rock Ashram is related by Mr. Veera from Kumbla, who was with the Master. One evening the Master asked for a bottle of arrack. The Master drank it all and asked for more. He drank seven bottles in quick succession. Veera, a hard drinker himself, could not believe his eyes. At the end of the seventh bottle the Master was suddenly thrown several feet into the air. Veera asked him how he managed to drink all this. Nityananda replied that he had not drunk anything—it was all for the spirit haunting the rock. He said the spirit was now satisfied and would not demand arrack or harm anyone in the future.

People going to the temple today will notice a small stone in front.

During worship, the arathi is taken around this stone as well after being waved before the Master's statue. Local belief held that a powerful spirit was located in the area. Older inhabitants of Kanhangad remember their parents saying that even during the day, people passing by would be affected if they did not pour a little arrack on the rock. As there was a beaten path providing a shortcut near the rock, people who did not know this often fell ill, occasionally seriously, if they passed by without the offering.

Although Nityananda spent considerable time in Kannangad between the years of 1925 and 1935, he was also often seen in other parts of the South Kanara district. In an area known as Kushalnagar, the actual compound bearing this name (a kilometer north of the Rock Ashram) was the scene of some of the Master's activities in 1931. He had constructed a stone roundtable there, at which he would sit and say, *"The Round Table Conference is on. So and so says this—Gandhi says that"* and so on, at the very time the Conference was in progress in London. When the curious checked the published accounts of the Round Table Conference as given in the newspapers, they found that these tallied exactly with what some had mistaken for imaginary prattle.

After construction of the Kanhangad caves was completed, sometime in 1933, the Master again embarked on a period of more frequent and often unpredictable travel. He could be found during this period in Vajreshwari, Gokarn, and Bombay in addition to Kanhangad and Ganeshpuri (his main bases). There is considerable confusion about his activities and movements outside of the instances related below, and there is a period during which no one knew his whereabouts. From various details I have been able to ascertain, it appears that he did not finally leave Kanhangad until 1940. In other words, though he was in Vajreshwari, Ganeshpuri and Kanheri for a few months, he was also available in Kanhangad, as my uncle had seen him there in the early part of 1940.

The following incident will perhaps serve to illustrate the confusion that developed concerning the Master's whereabouts during this period. One day as Nityananda sat under a tree near the Rock caves three local Muslims arrived and stood reverentially before him. As he had many Muslim devotees, this was not surprising. These three had just returned from their Haj pilgrimage to Mecca. The Master asked them what they had seen there. They replied, "We saw you there, Swamiji, and hence we are here to pay our homage." Nityananda averted his face, a faint smile on his lips.

Similarly, during his flying visits to Bombay (with a stop at Gokarn), he would be found in many places. Among these were the Chowpati sands, where Achutamama, a devotee from Kaup and Udipi, reports the following. The Master used to ask him to dig a small grave-like opening in the sands. The Master would then lie in the grave and ask to be completely buried in the sand. People would pass right over him. After a half hour or more, he would suddenly emerge from the sand and ask his companion to accompany him home. On one such occasion, the Master asked for a pit much deeper than usual and then did not emerge for over three hours. Achutamama got very nervous, but at the same time he was afraid to dig up the place. He was particularly worried since the pit was so much deeper that day. Finally at eight in the evening, after having been covered up for more than three hours, Nityananda emerged from the sands. When repeatedly asked what this was all about and where he had gone, he did not reply but casually hinted that he had been to Delhi for a little work.

It was also during this period that the Master was a regular visitor at Mrs. Muktabai's home in Bombay. Once when Mrs. Muktabai and her mother had gone to Nasik for a visit and a change of climate under medical advice, the Master managed the house in Bombay for Mrs. Muktabai's husband, attending to all the household chores himself.

Sometime in 1934 or 1935 it is assumed that he shifted his base to Akroli near Vajreshwari. He is reported to have carried out a number of construction tasks, including some repairs to the hot spring water tanks. He also built a charity hostel opposite the Vajreshwari temple, which is still standing though not well maintained. He repaired the nearby Nath Mandir as well as supervised the construction of a large well which is still the main source of water for the Vajreshwari people.

As usual, devotees soon came to know of the Master's new whereabouts. One faithful devotee from the Mangalore days, Sitarama Shenoy, was among the first to locate Nityananda at Akroli in Vajreshwari.

Nityananda teased him affectionately, *"So you have come chasing here as well?"* Mr. Shenoy, who reappears several times in this narrative, was instructed by the Master a short time later to open a restaurant opposite the Vajreshwari temple.

During this same period (circa 1934-35), Mrs. Muktabai along with several other Bombay devotees went to Vajreshwari for a picnic. As they finished their lunch, they were speaking of the Master and regretting how long it had been since they had seen him. Just then they saw a dark figure coming out from the neighboring jungle at the base of the Mandakini mountain. Mrs. Muktabai said, "Look, it is the Master!" but the others laughed and said she was just seeing what she wished to see. But as the figure came nearer, they saw that it was the Master. They could not believe their eyes, since it had been over three years since last they had seen him. They were very happy with this reunion, and for Mrs. Muktabai, Vajreshwari became a spot to be visited more often.

There were many other incidents during his stay in Vajreshwari, but the following quote from the late Mr. Krishnamurthy, journalist and biographer, who wrote a small brochure on Nityananda in 1957, bears reproducing:

> Two decades ago Nityananda lived for years on a tree in the heart of the Vajreshwari jungle…[Once a young man asked,] "Man cannot do the impossible, that is what a Yogi can do. Won't you awaken the kundalini in me?" Moved by the earnest tone of the young seeker, Nityananda touches his spinal cord. In a split second [he] experiences the dynamic charge of the kundalini. The confines of mortal hope blend with the confines of divine light. [He] feels a magnesium wire is burning in his head. It is at once the unfolding of a mystery and a wordless music. When kundalini returns to its spiritual cavern the light is put out and the flute broken. When one puts the eyes of logical reason to sleep he can grasp the mysterious flash of reality. For an intellectual statement of kundalini, we can dig up books from the stalls written with a classic tone and fullness. But, in our own day, Nityananda is the living emblem of the kundalini process. To him it is not a mental trap but a concept of action…. Nityananda opens the first window on our consciousness. From that moment, man no longer

feels time bound.... The entire greatness of Nityananda consists in the annihilation of time. The past becomes a closed memory. We cease to clutch to future passions. We live in the intuition of the second. It transforms man the great invalid into [man] the great knower.

Ganeshpuri: 1936-1961

The following stories of the Ganeshpuri days are arranged in a rough chronology; although it is rarely possible to positively date any detail of the Master's earthly life, most events can be placed within a five year range. Details of the move to Ganeshpuri are also not complete; the move was sudden and unplanned (or at least unannounced). It is generally believed that the goddess Vajreshwari directed the Master to Ganeshpuri. As mentioned in the introduction, Ganeshpuri had been a holy place even in ancient times and it was believed that Nityananda's presence there enhanced this holiness for the benefit of all concerned. Again, the stories reproduced here were either personally witnessed by me or were related to me by eyewitness sources. The reader should note that this section includes the time period already mentioned in the *Days of Peace and Happiness* chapter, which deals with my own relationship with the Master. The general time period covered here is from 1936 to 1961, with the final section, *The Mahasamadhi*, dealing with the events of August, 1961.

The Beginning: 1936

Nityananda moved to Ganeshpuri one fine morning in 1936. It may have been winter; he was wrapped in a checkered blanket. While it appears he told devotees at Vajreshwari that he was going to the

59

Bhimeshwar temple in Ganeshpuri, he is not reported to have spoken of settling there. The Ganeshpuri to which Nityananda came that day in 1936 was surrounded by jungle; the path of the present bus route was heavily wooded and wild beasts including tigers were still common. In addition to the Bhimeshwar temple, which was only accessible by an east/west footpath cutting across the Mandakini hill, the other major inhabitant was on the western side of the hill. There, a doctor had built a sanatorium with arrangements for piping the local hot spring water into specially constructed baths.

When Nityananda reached the Bhimeshwar temple that morning, Gangubai, then a young woman and wife of the old priest, would not allow him to enter, saying that it was a Hindu shrine. She had mistaken him for a Muslim. Nityananda did not force his way but retraced his steps to sit by the well. This well had clearly not been in use for many years, as it was over-grown with vegetation and covered with stones. The Master later described the stone growth as *shilajit*, and when the well was eventually cleared, this shilajit was eagerly collected by a number of Ayurvedic physicians.

One of the Vajreshwari devotees went in search of Nityananda when he had not returned by late afternoon. He was found sitting near the well. When it was learned that he had been turned away from the temple, the devotee hastened to explain to Gangubai who the Master was. They all apologized and within a couple of days constructed a small temporary structure for him on the western side of the temple. Visitors recall that there was hardly enough room for one person to crawl inside and sleep.

In front of Nityananda's room there was a massive old pipal tree that was home to many snakes and reptiles. As in Kanhangad, the Master apparently ordered all the snakes out. Swami Janananda told me that Kanhangad had been full of cobras, all of which obeyed Nityananda's vibrationary orders and left in the directions indicated, except one very large cobra that apparently committed suicide by laying its head on the railroad track outside the Ashram when a train passed by. Here in Ganeshpuri also, one large old cobra would not leave, but apparently insisted that it wanted samadhi at the hands of the Master. Thus the story is related of the day the Master told his devotees not to come near his little residence behind the temple, as the snake residing in the pipal tree was to be given samadhi that day. They don't know what he did, but they could approach him only in the afternoon when he said that the prayer of the old cobra had been granted. A few days later, the ancient pipal tree was cut down. Apparently the Master had arranged for some rituals to be performed before the sacred tree was cut, as there were festoons of threads about as well as sprinklings of *kum kum* (red powder used in rituals). At first the villagers were hesitant to cut the tree, fearing that they would be attacked by snakes; they began work only after Nityananda gave them his personal assurance of safety.

As word of the Master's arrival spread among the local villagers they began to assemble around his hut in the evenings on their way home. A large pot of rice porridge was prepared for the visitors and the Master would share a little with them every day. Devotees also began to visit Ganeshpuri as news of his new abode became known. He soon constructed the Ashram east of the temple tanks which is still in use by visiting devotees, particularly for changing after a bath in the hot springs.

In the beginning, devotees would stay only for the day, as there was no potable water until after the well was refitted, and the sulphur water of the hot springs was used for all purposes. This situation resulted in an interesting incident one hot April afternoon. The Master offered a visiting devotee a plate of rice mixed with the sauce of hot pickle; perhaps the Master knew she had not eaten lunch and this was the only food available. When he noticed that she was not eating, he asked her why. The devotee had not eaten the rice and pickle sauce because she knew there was no drinking water and she felt she could not drink the hot sulphur water after eating such a spicy mixture. So in response to the Master's question, she replied that there was no water to drink. With no hesitation, the Master said, *"Drink rain water."* She remained silent, but since the sky was blue and the sun very bright, she did not understand his meaning and still did not eat. Within five minutes a thunder cloud appeared as if from nowhere; rain poured down for twenty minutes. The Master said *"You were waiting for water. Go and get as much as you want."* The devotee did so, placing a number of vessels in the open and collecting enough rain water to satisfy her own needs and to store some for the Master.

Soon after this, three rooms on the southern side of the temple were constructed; these were the beginnings of the "old Ashram." Nityananda's room, with a small cement platform in front, was in the center. The rooms flanking his were both fully walled but in his own room the walls were only about seven feet high with a sliding door barely two feet above the platform level forming the entrance. Perhaps he did not want any secrecy about him. In the second phase of the old Ashram's construction (about 1943) the area in front of these three rooms was paved with stones. Prior to that he would meet devotees either in the building near the tanks, or in the inner quadrangle of the temple.

Directly in front of the newly constructed rooms there were only trees and jungle, with the only road to the Ashram being the winding private road leading to the neighboring sanatorium. The caretakers of the sanatorium objected to devotees getting off the bus in front of their gate and using their path to go to Nityananda's Ashram, and began to charge the visitors a fee. This practice continued until one day there was an argument between the visitors and the caretakers during which some blows were exchanged. At this point, the devotees took the problem to Nityananda for solution.

After listening to them, Nityananda told the local villagers to call for laborers. About fifty men reported for work the next morning. They were asked to cut the trees in front of the Ashram all the way to the bus route and then to commence construction of a road. In both these operations Nityananda was an active participant, so much so that many visitors during this period found it difficult to pick him out from among the laborers working in the jungle or on the road.

In a very short time the road to the Ashram was ready for use; State Transport buses still use this road when carrying devotees to Ganeshpuri. Soon thereafter, the District Magistrate and the District Forest Officer received a report about the unauthorized clearing of trees and construction of the road. The local forest ranger was a devotee, so he came to forewarn the Master that a complaint had been received and that it was an offense according to regulations, since no permission had been obtained from the required authorities. Nityananda, however, told the ranger, *"You are a government servant; the government pays you to do your job and so you must do what the government expects of you when such a complaint is received."* The ranger felt crestfallen since he had wished to be of service to the Master. However, when he actually wrote his report, he instinctively stressed that the forest had been cleared and the road constructed for public welfare and not for private profit; that with Nityananda settling in Ganeshpuri, a large influx of devotees from Bombay could be expected, and it was necessary for them to have access to the Ashram;

that visiting devotees from Vajreshwari needed access to the Bhimeshwar temple, and that in light of all this, the clearing and road construction should have been a project undertaken by a local body of government. Therefore, by this act, the government had been saved considerable expense and effort, and a much needed facility was painlessly acquired in a very short time.

After reading this report, the District Collector and the District Forest Officer (both foreigners) came to Ganeshpuri one morning in 1937. Parking their car well beyond where the Bhadrakali temple now stands, they walked until they were near the mango tree, about 100 yards from the open Ashram. The Master was seated on the cement platform facing them. As soon as they came near the mango tree on his left, he turned 180 degrees and sat facing his own room, with his back to the approaching visitors. The moment this happened, the officials also turned and went back to their car. The Collector remarked to his subordinates that though he was well paid by the government he was rarely moved by any charitable considerations, while this man who possessed only a loincloth was striving for the benefit of the local poor, and saving the local authorities a lot of time and money in the bargain. "No further action" was the decision on the report. One is reminded of the Gawne incident in Kanhangad.

The Old Ashram: 1936-1950

One afternoon in the late thirties, a visitor was taking leave of the Master after spending a few hours in Ganeshpuri. He was planning to follow the footpath that cut diagonally through the woods to the Vajreshwari temple. As he left, the Master told him not to look back until he reached the temple. Along the way he found a cobra in the middle of the path but did not retrace his steps or look back; he simply waited until it moved away. Soon after this, he heard what sounded like someone whispering incessantly behind him. Controlling his curiosity in order to comply with the Master's directive, he did not look back; but as he was approaching the temple and could see the spire, he involuntarily turned, not being able to stand the bombardment of the constant whisper. He reported seeing a gigantic figure with folded arms standing in the middle of the river saying *japa* (mantra repetitions). It was this he had heard as a constant whisper. The sight so shook him that he was not himself, although he somehow managed to reach the temple.

Once inside it, he was in a dazed semi-conscious condition for nearly two hours, and later had to be hospitalized. It took him about two months to return to normalcy.

There are numerous other examples of the Master's watchfulness. He always advised the devotees not to venture out alone at night. One night Mrs. Muktabai, not knowing the time, got up soon after midnight and went for a bath in the hot spring tanks. As soon as she entered, she saw two unusually handsome youths who rushed from the baths and disappeared inside the temple. Feeling a bit nervous, she hurried back to the Ashram to seek the Master. He admonished her for disobeying his instructions about not going out alone at that late hour. She replied apologetically that she had not been aware of the time, but wanted to know who the young lads were. The Master replied that they were *sanatkumars* (four sons of Brahma born of his mind alone).

Years later, in 1965, when I spoke with older devotees from this era, one of the things I learned from them was that the young Master would often repeat the expression "tortoise *drishti*" (sight). When asked for my interpretation of this phrase, I explained that as far as could be made out from the Master's personality and from the subsequent experiences of devotees, it might have indicated that he was constantly thinking of them, of their welfare and their evolution. It is said that while birds hatch their eggs by physical warmth, the mother tortoise climbs to the sands, lays her eggs, covers them and returns to the sea. But all the while, she thinks of the eggs and so helps them to hatch by her constant attention. So I explained that the Master must have been saying that he would be protecting the devotees like a mother in all respects, and that he would be accepting full responsibility for their spiritual evolution. Many of the stories, not only those that immediately follow, illustrate this "tortoise drishti."

On another occasion a devotee was engaged in performing some seva to the Master in the original Ashram and was asked to retire about midnight. On his way to the tanks for a wash, he saw a huge muddy footprint on the stones near the *Nandi* (statue of the bull of Shiva). Though a man of courage, he was shaken by the sight, and rushed inside. The Master immediately asked him, *"Did you bow before the footprint?"* He quickly returned and bowed before the footprint, but could not get the Master to say any more about it.   On another occasion, the Master is reported to have said that there were many sages around the old Ashram—a regular assembly of sages *(rishi mandal).*

Perhaps it is for these reasons that the Master used to say that the water in the kunds was *koti teertha*—very holy. This phrase is used to indicate waters in which many holy persons had bathed through the ages and in the proximity of which many saints had meditated. Throughout his stay at Ganeshpuri, the Master would ask all visitors to bathe in the kunds; even the oldest devotees, on arrival, were asked whether they had bathed in the kunds.

During the dark mornings also, he maintained a watch on the devotees until they returned to the Ashram after their bath. Once Madhumama (Mr. Madhav Nayak), an old-time devotee who sometimes cooked for the Master, was surprised to see Nityananda near the entrance as he entered the Ashram at 4:30 A.M. after his bath. Just as he entered, the Master asked him whether he had "seen." Madhumama, of course, did not understand. The Master then pointed to a tiger sitting under the mango tree, only about 20 to 30 yards away. The Master had been watching for his devotee's safety.

Mr. Rajgopal Bhat, a regular weekend visitor for two decades, told me of a similar incident that occurred in 1949. He had brought his family to Bombay for the first time, and not having secured accommodations was advised by the Master to stay with Mr. Gandhi in the village of Ganeshpuri. The next morning he got up at 3:00 A.M. and was proceeding to the kunds when he felt that he was being followed. He could also see a faint light behind him. Thinking of the Master, he never looked back but kept on walking. As he reached the site where the Bhadrakali temple is now situated, the light disappeared and the feeling ceased. He finished his bath but never told the Master, nor did he think about it. That evening, when Mr. Gandhi went to the Ashram, the Master told him that a tiger had followed Mr. Bhat that morning but that his faith in the Master acted as a protective shield.

At another time during these very early days, Bhagawan Mistry, the contractor-mason who was in charge of all Ashram construction work, came shouting one evening that he had been bitten by a cobra. He was suffering excruciating pain. Nityananda told him to sit in a certain place, then asked one of the devotees to get a bottle of balm. When it was brought, the bewildered Mistry was instructed to rub the balm on Nityananda's leg. After a while, Mistry was told to go to sleep. When he awoke the next morning, he was fully recovered.

Nityananda sometimes intervened even more dramatically for the welfare of his devotees. Dr. Deodhar narrated the following to me.

Sitarama Shenoy, the Mangalore devotee mentioned earlier as finding the Master in Vajreshwari, was hospitalized after a severe heart attack and was advised to observe strict bedrest. His family considered taking him to Ganeshpuri, but the doctors warned that he might not survive the strain of travel. However, the family decided to take the risk; they drove Shenoy to Ganeshpuri. He was assisted from the car and helped to lie in front of the Master in the old Ashram, which was not yet ready for occupation. The Master took him by the hand and half led, half dragged him to the river. When they reached the river, Nityananda splashed some water on the face of the ailing man, telling him he was quite all right and could walk back independently. He did so. To the great pleasure of his family and the great surprise of his doctors, he was completely restored. Shortly thereafter he opened the restaurant opposite the Vajreshwari temple at the Master's bidding, where he continued until his death in 1954. The restaurant is still run by members of his family.

Achutamama was sitting alone with the Master one afternoon in the late thirties when the Master announced that Narayan Maharaj would be arriving soon. The devotee was skeptical, since he thought the Maharaj was in Khedgaon. The Master, however, said he was in Vajreshwari and on his way to the Ashram. Less than five minutes later a car was heard stopping outside and Narayan Maharaj arrived. He had a bath in the kunds before approaching the Master, asking to be cured of his skin disorder. Nityananda said, *"The inside is pure; why are you bothered about the outside?"* That night after the Maharaj was gone, Nityananda said cryptically of him, *"Everything was ready for Narayan Maharaj. The bed was made and his head was about to touch the pillow, when he suddenly got up."* He did not explain further, but the reference could have been to the high stage of attainment the saint had reached at one time. On the same occasion the Master said that *datta devata siddhi* lasted 14 years and thereafter fresh efforts were needed to have it renewed. For divine wisdom (*jnana*) no such limitation existed; it was infinite.

Some time in 1938, a man destined to be a long-time devotee made his first visit to Ganeshpuri. While most visitors arrived at the Ashram by bus, Golikeri Lakshman Rao had recently won a Goa lottery and was a rich man. He rode in a taxi all the way, bearing a fruit casket. The Master accepted him as well as his fruit. After two or three visits, Nityananda asked Rao to come on a particular date (near the end of 1938) so they could both go on a *teertha-yatra* (pilgrimage to holy waters). Rao came with a taxi on the chosen date. The villagers gathered to plead with Nityananda not to leave them, falling at his feet. He told them they should fall at Rao's feet and much to his embarrassment they did so. Nityananda motioned to him to accept them, and in a short while they began their journey.

At the train station, Nityananda insisted on third-class tickets despite Rao's protestations that he would be glad to purchase first-class accommodations. Poona was their first stop. That night, they took a hotel room with only one bed, again at Nityananda's insistence. Further, Nityananda refused to sleep in the bed and insisted that Rao do so despite his pleas and protestations. Nityananda slept on the ground with only a cloth (*chaddar*) as a blanket. The next day they went to Alandi, where Nityananda encouraged Rao to follow his usual mode of prayer and worship. Thus, Rao proceeded to the river for his bath then sat in front of the samadhi of Jnaneshwar for worship. The Master simply stood straight with his hands at his sides for a few seconds at each of the four corners of the shrine and then left allowing Rao to worship in his own manner.

The next stop was to have been Pandarpur, but Rao got a severe attack of malaria that night and asked Nityananda for permission to return to Bombay. The Master had no objection but asked Rao to leave his chaddar. Rao protested that he would gladly buy a new one, but on the insistence of Nityananda he yielded, and then returned to Bombay.

Nityananda traveled on to Pandarpur and a few other places, then returned to Bombay. From there, he did not return directly to Ganeshpuri, but spent several months in the Kanheri Caves at Borivli during late 1938 or early 1939. Adjoining his cave was another where a guru was daily lecturing his disciples on Vedantic philosophy. The main theme of the lectures was the inconsequential and transitory aspect of the human body. The disciples were therefore exhorted to ignore the body with all of its charms and afflictions. As fate would have it, the mentor was one day bitten by a snake hidden in the foliage nearby. He was obviously in great agony and was giving visible and audible expression to his physical suffering. The disciples were greatly distressed over the unfortunate condition of their teacher and approached Nityananda for help. While the Master's mercy knew no bounds, he nevertheless chuckled and asked if they had forgotten all the teachings requiring them to ignore the body and its afflictions. However he directed them to splash a little water from the nearby pond on the wound; this done, the teacher recovered immediately and came to offer his salutations to the Master.

As mentioned earlier in the case of Sitarama Shenoy, devotees would find Nityananda and gather around him no matter where he was staying. During this time in Kanheri also, devotees came to him. Mrs. Muktabai, who was deeply attached to the Master, was a frequent visitor. It appears that the Master's watchfulness also continued regardless of the location. Mrs. Muktabai relates that once she arrived rather late in the evening and in her haste, found that she had lost her way. Just as she was beginning to feel quite nervous, an old asthmatic man appeared and offered to show her the way. As they neared the ashram, the old man began to lag behind her; when the ashram was in sight and she turned to thank him, he was nowhere to be seen. When she arrived, Nityananda reprimanded her for traveling in that area so late, as it was known to be a dangerous region.

During this period, another of the caves was occupied by a sanyasi who was a Maha Kali worshipper. Every day after his worship he would bring the arathi he had waved before Maha Kali's photograph and wave it before the Master. There was apparently no reaction from the Master, who told the devotees that it was done simply because of the sanyasi's feeling of devotion.

On one of their last visits to Kanheri, just before the Master's return to Ganeshpuri, the Master told the devotees that it was not enough that they came to see him there; he urged them to see the wonderful rock-cut caves, complete with arrangements for the collection and storage of water and other facilities constructed by yogis and sanyasis centuries ago.

Nityananda returned to Ganeshpuri after these few months in the Kanheri caves. Mr. Rao saw the Master there in 1939; on this occasion

Rao again suffered a severe attack of malaria. In the delirium brought about by his high fever, he began to talk of an incident in his youth in which he had been given some sandwiches as prasad by the Muslim sage Baba Jan, but had thrown them away. When Nityananda heard this, he shook Rao and asked him to repeat what he had said. After listening to the story again, Nityananda went to the food storage shelves, opened several tins of savory mixture and other food, and mixed the contents together on a piece of newspaper. He brought the huge helping to the ailing Rao and exhorted him to eat. Although Rao was very ill, he dutifully ate all he was given and then immediately fell asleep. When he awoke he was fully recovered. He also felt that he had atoned for the insult of throwing away the prasad of a saint.

Swami Janananda told of a visit he made to Ganeshpur in 1941, seeking guidance from the Master about some financial difficulties and some construction questions at the Kanhangad Ashram. Upon arrival in Ganeshpuri, he was immediately told to sit down. Within minutes a taxi arrived, apparently in answer to a summons from the Ashram—a very unusual occurrence in those days. The Master asked Swami Janananda to wait for him because he would be back very soon, then departed in the taxi. At exactly the same time the next morning, the Master returned in the same taxi. He told Swami Janananda to return to Kanhangad; funds had been arranged, and the needed construction directions had been given to a local devotee.

Swami Janananda returned to Kanhangad via the usual modes of travel, involving several trains and buses. The local devotee confirmed that Nityananda had been there and had left money and instructions. It should be noted that even under the best modern conditions, including the new Netravati bridge, it is still impossible to complete a round trip between Bombay and Kanhangad by taxi in twenty-four hours.

As Nityananda was not involved in garnering disciples or organizing a Mission, so also he had no sense of ego about his own following or lack of it.

This one is not flattered because some important persons have visited or depressed if someone who used to come has not turned up.

Often people who were committed to a particular teacher would visit Ganeshpuri; the Master would always steer them back to their own teacher. One morning devotees of Shirdi Sai Baba came before Nityananda in the old Ashram, but even before all of them could enter, the Master was heard shouting, *"Go to Shirdi. Is the old man sitting there different from here?"* What the Master meant was that Shirdi Sai Baba was quite capable of solving their problem and being his devotees they should not change their loyalties for a temporary purpose.

Dr. Deodhar told me of a similar situation involving an affluent family in Bhiwandi known as the Bhiwandiwalla brothers, who were devotees of Narayan Maharaj of Khedgaon. On hearing that Nityananda had settled in Ganeshpuri, they went there, but even before they entered the Ashram, Nityananda shouted, *"Go to Narayan Maharaj."* Nevertheless they insisted on coming, but Nityananda never spoke to them until after Narayan Maharaj attained samadhi. On their next visit after this, he began to speak to the Bhiwandiwallas; they had many pleasant experiences and became devout visitors to Ganeshpuri.

Another devotee was popularly known in the Ashram as Raddiwalla. It was understood that he had lost a flourishing business just before the war and had come to Ganeshpuri to seek Nityananda's blessing. On the afternoon of that visit, the Master kept repeating the word *raddi* (waste material). This expression started working on the man who had lost his fortune; try as he might, he could not rid his mind of the word. It was still ringing in his ears the next day as he walked through the city only to come upon an auction of raddi. He purchased it at once, and was able to sell the lot at a profit in a very short time. Within a few months he was well on his way toward recouping his previous losses. From then on he was known as Raddiwalla. [11]

---

[11]"Walla" is a suffix meaning "person in charge of."

He was a frequent visitor at Ganeshpuri, often bringing his whole family, including the children. He was particularly anxious to have the Master's physical blessing; at times he would take the liberty of respectfully holding the Master's hand, raising it and placing it on the head of the relative he wished to have blessed. Not unnaturally, this provoked some feelings of envy, particularly among the older devotees who had known Nityananda in Mangalore. One day, Raddwalla took his leave after garnering several benedictions as usual with the Master's hand placed on the head of every member of his family. The remaining devotees finally questioned the Master, wondering why they had never been so favored, even after so many years; indeed, in Mangalore they had been told not even to prostrate themselves since prayers offered internally would reach him. Nityananda rebuked them, saying, *"Is blessing (ashirvad) given by placing the hand on the head? Ashirvad is an internal transmission and not an external demonstration."*

One day in the old Ashram, the Master was complaining of tiredness. Mrs. Muktabai was on very familiar terms with the Master, so she ventured to say that she was surprised at this, since he rarely left the Ashram, spending most of his time resting on the floor of his room or on the bench outside. He cryptically replied, *"Yes, but the devotees remember—don't they?"* He repeated this on another occasion to another devotee.

> *Once one is established in infinite consciousness, one becomes silent, and though knowing everything, goes about as if he does not know anything. Though he might be doing a lot of things in several places, to all outward appearance, he will remain as if he does nothing.*

A devotee tells of one of his first visits to Ganeshpuri. After saluting the Master, he and his wife were sitting a little distance away from him in the old Ashram. Some of the other visitors were discussing the building of a small school in the local area. Thinking this would be a good opportunity for contributing, the devotee got up and placed a thousand rupee note on the plate at the foot of the Master's bench. He returned immediately to his seat and was amazed to see his single note replaced by several smaller denomination bills. His wife also noted this with surprise, but neither of them spoke.

The Master was fond of the expression "automatic." He once told me that there was no point in planning or plotting to do this or that. *"When God wills it, who can hinder?"* he said to me.

A Kerala devotee relates his dismay when, in 1949, a renowned astrologer told him that his young wife would soon die due to an affliction from Saturn. The distraught man rushed to Ganeshpuri to seek the Master's aid and benediction, since he had two young children to raise. When he arrived, there were only two or three other people there sitting before Nityananda. As soon as he sat down to join them, Nityananda turned his head and said, *"Saturn is there, but God is also there."* The young man stayed on at the Ashram, and he was instructed to undergo certain strange and inexplicable experiences. He underwent these in strict obedience to the instructions issued. The day predicted for the calamity came and passed without incident, and the devotee was sent home.

One morning in the old Ashram at Ganeshpuri some devotees sat facing the Master, who was on his bench with his legs outstretched. At about 10 A.M., three stalwart sanyasis entered the Ashram from the old entrance behind Nityananda. One of them carried a large and brightly polished *trishula* (trident). They stood quietly behind Nityananda, perhaps expecting him to look back or otherwise receive them. The Master made no sign or sound. The visitors began to get restless and the devotees, who were perforce spectators, were feeling a bit uncomfortable. Then the person holding the trishula forcefully planted it in midair and it remained standing there. Still Nityananda did not look back or move his head at all, but each time he looked to the right from the corner of his eye, the trishula swayed gently. After a minute or so, Nityananda shook his outstretched foot, and the trishula fell with a bang. The sanyasis saluted and sought permission to stay on in the Ashram. During their three day stay they told the Master's devotees that they were with a powerful guru in the Himalayan region, but that they were prepared to concede that Nityananda was *Matsyendranath* (a great leader of the Nath order) himself. They showed h m great respect and affection during their stay and left after seeking his bless ng.

In about 1942, Mr. Kamath (author of the first English version of the *Chidakash Gita*) [12], was spending *Shivaratri* (festival of Shiva) night n Ganeshpuri with a friend. They were staying in the rooms opposite the hot water tanks as the main Ashram was not yet ready. They stayed awake until midnight, when they had a bath and went inside the pitch dark temple of Bhimeshwar with the help of a torch light. To their shock, they found the Master standing there with one foot on the linga. He spoke in Konkani (Mr. Kamath's mother tongue): *"Shiva is gone, Shiva is gone."* It is to be assumed that for Shiva to have gone he must first have come.

Once Mrs. Mutkabai asked the Master whether he could see God. He replied, *"More clearly than you can be seen."*

Devotees often raised questions concerning the need for the Master's physical presence; he always assured them that physical contact was not necessary.

> *This one is here, there, and everywhere; there is not a pin-hole where this one will not be found.*

An incident in the life of G.L. Rao illustrates this point very literally. Rao was devoutly attached to the Master and very generous with the wealth he had obtained by good fortune (it may be recalled that he had won a sizeable lottery), but the war had reversed his fortunes; he had lost everything. In response to the Master's request, another devotee had provided him with a place to sleep in his warehouse. Rao would sometimes think sadly of the extent to which he had been reduced; now he did not even own a picture of the Master to wave an incense stick before. That night he dreamed that the Master told him to look at the wall just above his pillow for a hole created by a pulled-out nail. He told Rao that if he waved incense before the pinhole, it would reach him. For the rest of his stay in the warehouse, Rao performed the cere-

---

[12] Collection of Nityananda's sayings and aphorisms as taken down by devotees. A new English language edition is soon to be released as a companion volume to this book.

mony before the pinhole. On a subsequent visit to Ganeshpuri, the Master smiled and told him that he was enjoying the fragrance of the incense.

Once a group of six or seven people came from Saurashtra to pay their respects to the Master in the old Ashram. When bowing before the Master one of them shivered slightly and shook. As they were leaving, a devotee called that particular person aside and asked him why he had shivered. The visitor replied that he had seen the Master in a cave near Saurashtra and that caused an emotional upsurge. After they left, the devotee addressed the Master: "How bogus some of these people are. One of the visitors said that he saw you in a cave in Saurashtra. How is it possible?" The Master answered simply, *"Everything is possible."*

To the Master, this was always clear; to the devotees, it often needed restating. When Madhumama was asked to go to Badrinath by the Master some time in the mid-fifties he stopped over at Rishikesh. There he was approached by a tall South Indian, who warned him in Kanarese: "Don't eat anything offered by any sanyasi on the way to Badrinath. Anything offered from a temple may be eaten." Madhumama was mystified, both by the message and by the fact that the stranger had known he understood Kanarese and known that he was traveling to Badrinath. He turned to question him, but the stranger had disappeared. When he returned from Badrinath, he told the other devotees that when he bowed at Kedarnath, he felt as if his head was touching the Master's body. Again, some of the devotees laughed, disbelieving this experience. The Master replied, *"There is no need to doubt his experience. The* Munda *(body without the head) is in Kedarnath and* Runda *(head without the body) is in Pashupathinath."* According to this the body of Shiva is in Kedarnath and the head in Pashupathinath. Hence feeling the touch of the body in Kedarnath was possible.

The following story illustrates how closely Nityananda watched over his devotees and the often unusual methods he employed to garner benefit for them. M. Hegde, a young relative of Sitarama

Shenoy, became a regular visitor to Ganeshpuri soon after the outbreak of the second World War, when he came to Bombay from Mangalore. The Master would sometimes permit him to prepare tea for
him. In Bombay, the young man joined the Naval Dockyard as an ap-
prentice, receiving a small stipend. After a few years in the appren-
ticeship program, he could expect to be offered a permanent job in the
Dockyard. During one of his visits to the jungle Ashram, Nityananda
questioned him closely: Did he wish to improve his prospects? Had he
read in the newspapers of the Bevin Boy's Training Program in the
United Kingdom that the government was sponsoring? Hegde replied
that he had read about it but understood that quotas had been set by
province; thus he feared he would not be considered eligible as he did
not strictly belong to the Bombay province. The Master told him not to
view things from such a narrow angle out of diffidence, but to put in an
application. Hegde did so and was among those selected. During the
medical examination, however, the local medical officer objected to
his applying through Bombay and therefore declared him medically
unfit. Hegde hurried to Ganeshpuri. Nityananda again told him not to
use such narrow thinking; was there not a Surgeon General to whom
an appeal could be made? The young man wrote to the Surgeon
General and was asked to appear for an interview. Seeing the hefty
young man, the official was puzzled by the "unfit" ruling. The local
doctor was sent for and asked to explain what exactly was wrong with
the candidate. There being no satisfactory explanation, the doctor
received a warning, and Hegde was approved for the program.

Soon after Hegde arrived in the U.K. for the year of training, he became friendly with a local girl. The two often went to the parks in their
free time. On one such occasion, Hegde suddenly saw an apparition of
the Master before him. His face was very stern and he seemed to say,
"Was it for this that you were sent to this place?" The apparition disappeared. Hegde recalls he was sweating profusely even though the
weather was quite cold and he was wearing an overcoat. In the meantime, he was not sure what contorted expression his face had assumed
as a result of the experience, because the girl had run away and the two
never met again. This part of his life in the U.K. became a closed chapter.

On his return to India, Hegde traveled to Ganeshpuri to ask the Master what he should do now as he did not wish to go back to the Dockyard. The Master asked him if he had any suits. Hearing that he did, the
Master then instructed him to wear one of them, and walk up and

down a major commercial street from 10 A.M. to 5 P.M. This was a tall order but the young devotee resolved to carry it out to the letter. He returned home at 5 in the evening quite tired and began to wonder how he would get a job by pacing up and down the road. Nevertheless his faith was firm; the next day he went out again. By 11:30 he was quite tired and began to stare aimlessly at the hoardings outside the Macropolo shop. Out of the corner of his eye, he saw a foreigner entering the shop. When the foreigner left the store some time later, he was surprised to see Hegde still staring at the hoarding, and asked the young man what he was looking for. Hegde answered truthfully that he was looking for a job. The stranger asked his qualifications and whether he was prepared to go to Calcutta that night. When Hegde said he would be able to go, the foreigner took him to his office in the Lakshmi Building and gave him orders for a reasonably well-paid job as well as money to travel that night to Calcutta. Hegde caught the first train to go to Ganeshpuri. He was still 100 yards from the Ashram when he heard Nityananda shouting that he must turn back to the station immediately if he intended to catch the Calcutta train. So, with a grateful salutation from a distance, Hegde set out on his new job.

My mother had been among those devotees who visited the Master in South Kanara, beginning in 1919. She stopped doing so in the early twenties, and in 1924 she had the darshan of Swami Siddharud in Hubli. She was very impressed with him and brought back a large book listing many miracles attributed to him. After my own connection with Nityananda was established in 1943, I wrote about this rediscovery to my mother, inviting her to visit Ganeshpuri. I had written that if I was not available my uncle in Bombay could escort her. So it was that in February 1944, my mother accompanied my uncle and his family to Ganeshpuri, where they joined the other devotees gathered in the open area opposite the Master. With his characteristic brevity, he asked her, *"How long?"* My mother was unprepared for this greeting, and mumbled, "Perhaps twenty years." *"No,"* came the reply, *"It is twenty-two. Anyway, where is Siddharud now?"* My mother replied that he was no more. *"Where is he gone then? Can't you see him if you close your eyes?"* When this was confirmed, he asked again: *"Where is he gone then?"*

That night the party stayed in the room nearest to the hot baths. In the evening, the Master came to sit with them, but was silent most of the time. One of the ladies asked about his silence, and another suggested that since it was just sunset, perhaps he was meditating, implying that sunset was a particularly appropriate time for meditation. They were speaking within the hearing of all in the room, and the Master spoke at once, *"All that was over in the mother's womb."*

In greeting my mother as he did, the Master casually confirmed his ability to see across spaces not ordinarily traversable. Some devotees would then raise the question: If events could be foretold, could all unpleasant events be avoided? There does not appear to be a simple answer. Many devotees tell stories in which seemingly inexplicable behavior was demanded by the Master, only to learn later that certain discomforts and inconveniences had been averted by that behavior. An example involving a housewife devotee in Mangalore has already been given, in the *Early Years* chapter. In another such instance, a couple who were devotees arrived in Ganeshpuri one morning and occupied a room opposite the temple. After finishing their bath and arranging to cook a meal, a part of which was as usual to be offered to the Master, they prepared to go for his darshan. However, as they stepped out of the room, they saw the Master hurrying across the compound toward them, shouting that they must leave immediately. Their pleas were ignored and the cooking had to be stopped at once. They did not understand, but packed and obeyed. A bus was just leaving and they easily made the rail connection at Bassein. Just as they were entering their flat, a fierce gale started blowing, rattling the shutters and windows; a terrific storm was brewing. There was considerable damage in their area; railway connections were severed between Virar and Borivli for a week. In fact, the couple traveled by the last bus and the last train; otherwise they would have been trapped in Ganeshpuri for some ten days. There were many such instances; it was as if the devotion shown by devotees who came to visit Nityananda saved them from suffering undue inconvenience.

Another example of an apparent hardship proving to be a blessing upon closer examination involved a regularly visiting devotee and his wife. The couple had come to Ganeshpuri for a couple of days, then after offering due salutations they hired a horse-drawn tonga to take them to Vajreshwari. As the wife was climbing into the tonga, she fell, fracturing her ankle. The husband ran back to the Master, who said that the woman need not be taken to the hospital but to a bonesetter. He gave him the name and address of a bonesetter in Bombay. After they left, a friend who stayed behind asked the Master how such a thing could happen right in Ganeshpuri. The Master replied, *"She has young children. A fatal accident would have meant distress for them."* A fatal accident had apparently been avoided.

Nityananda's broad and deep understanding of events was often beyond the ken of his devotees. Time after time, someone would express concern or sorrow about an event only to have the Master explain, sometimes with a little exasperation, that the surface appearance was not necessarily correct. The two examples above illustrate this, but an even more dramatic example follows.

Once early in the fifties, Dr. Deodhar recalls seeing two cars arrive. Servants carrying bedding rolls emerged from one of them and entered the Ashram through the rear door. It was the Bhiwandiwalla family and it appeared that they were going to stay for a couple of days. The family members emerged from the other car and entered the Ashram through the main entrance. One of them moved awkwardly as he was carrying a child in his extended arms; the child was inert and appeared very ill. In less than ten minutes, the servants came out with the bedding rolls, the family emerged from the Ashram with the child still held in the same manner, and they all left. The doctor was intrigued; he sought out B. Mistry, who was the only other person present in the Ashram at the time, and asked him what had happened. Mistry said that the child had been unconscious. It was suffering from a severe case of pneumonia and had not opened its eyes for three days. The family brought the child before the Master and asked that the child's eyes be opened. The Master passed his hand over the face of the child and the eyes opened; however, as his hand returned over the face, the eyes closed once again. The Master told the family to perform the last rites—the child was dead.

B. Mistry was quite familiar with the Master, having undertaken all the construction work at the Ashram from the early days, so he felt emboldened to commiserate with him about this event. Mistry said it was unfortunate that the child passed away in the Ashram; that if it had to happen, it would have been better if it had occurred elsewhere and not in the Master's presence. The Master rebuked him, saying, *"What do you know or understand about these matters? This is the fourth time the same child has come out of the same mother's womb and it has been seeking mukti. It has been wanting freedom but karmic law has been dragging it down again and again for manifestation in the same family.*

*Its intense desire has been fulfilled now and it won't have to come
again."* In response to inquiries by Dr. Deodhar, the family confirmed
that this was the fourth child. The three previous children had all died
shortly after birth and this fourth had also died, but only after darshan
of the Master.

Another strange case relating to a sick child is reported from this era
at Ganeshpuri. A couple from Bombay had their first child late in life.
This beloved son contracted smallpox when he was only a few weeks
old. They brought the child straight to Ganeshpuri to the Master, and
placed him at the feet of the Master in full view of the many devotees
gathered that evening. The Master apparently did not approve of the
way in which they had entered, especially since there were many other
children present. He asked that the sick child be removed, and that the
parents also leave immediately. He then went into his room in the
center of the hall, and was rarely seen for the next ten days, after which
he had a bath. A small number of skin eruptions were discovered on his
body. The child, of course, was cured.

Dr. Deodhar tells the following tale. There is a small Shiva shrine on
his family's jungle estate near Panvel. Swami Ramananda was
installed there to perform the daily rituals. Every weekend he came to
the Deodhar house to collect his weekly rations and other supplies.
During one such visit, the family members were discussing the
possibility of unearthing a basement that they believed lay below their
house. Swami Ramananda affirmed that there was a basement and he
said there was some gold as well, being guarded by a snake. He offered
to send the snake away and secure the gold for them. When the doctor
replied that they were not seeking gold, only a basement, the Swami
reasoned that after he had unearthed the basement and secured the
gold, the family could do as they liked with it. Therefore he remained
with them after the weekend to supervise the digging operation.

After two days of careful digging to considerable depth, no basement was visible. The family wanted to close up the excavation in
order not to endanger the building. Swami Ramananda asked for just
one more day before abandoning the whole project. That night he
stayed in the trench; his breathing was so deep and loud that it could be
heard inside the house. He climbed out in the early hours of the next
morning, telling Dr. Deodhar that they should fill in the excavation.

He added angrily that the "langotiwalla" had done something and that he was going to see about it. When asked to explain, he said he was referring to Nityananda of Ganeshpuri.

The Doctor was astonished to hear Swami Ramananda speak as if he knew the Master, since Nityananda was believed to have been in the South all along, and in recent years in Bombay. But the Swami said he had known Nityananda many many years ago in Rishikesh and that even then he had been a very powerful saint. The Master had been known to lie on the Ganges near the shore for days on end without food or water. Further, the Swami explained that his siddhis were being blinded and that was why nothing was visible; it was not that the basement and gold did not exist.

Dr. Deodhar was interested in meeting Nityananda since he had heard a great deal about him from his patients and also because he was himself a seeker, often visiting saints in Maharashtra. He decided to accompany Swami Ramananda to Ganeshpuri, but after they missed a connection in Thana, the doctor returned home. Swami Ramananda promised to tell him the outcome of the meeting.

Two days later, Swami Ramananda made his report. He had received a severe admonition from Nityananda: *"This is the third time you have used your siddhis in recent years. There is a long way to be covered in spiritual quests and you ought to know by now that you cannot cover that distance by misusing these powers for egocentric purposes. In any case, why did you try it out again in Panvel?"* Swami Ramananda, who had been all boldness when planning his meeting with Nityananda, saying he was going to demand the reason for the blinding of his siddhis, explained to Deodhar that he had become meek as a lamb before the Master, saying that he was only trying to express his sense of gratitude at Panvel. Nityananda admonished him again saying that this was not the way to do so. He then directed him to go to a spot on the Narmada River and there continue his practices. Ramananda left for the Narmada immediately after conveying this message to Dr. Deodhar and was never seen again. Incidently, this experience proved to be the final jolt Dr. Deodhar needed to send him to Nityananda, and he would always say afterward that there was no other like the Master.

Incidents such as this one serve to increase the confusion about Nityananda's age, background, and movements. For instance, the only information known about his visits to the northern regions is a general indication that he traveled in the north between the ages of 12 and 16 or so, after leaving his foster father in Benares. In addition to Swami Ramananda, many other witnesses are certain that they met Nityananda at times and in places that seem (at the very least) to stretch conventional notions of time and space. There are reports such as the one made to me in 1944 by a Mr. M.S. Rao of Udipi who remembers Nityananda saying that when the Ananteshwar temple was under construction (it is much older than the Krishna temple and is by far the oldest in the area), he used to sit on the site and that at that time he had a beard and matted locks.

The Old Ashram: 1950-1956

Late one evening in 1950, devotees were sitting outside the Ashram on the western side. The Master sat in front of them on a raised area that was enclosed by a small ledge. Behind him was a drop of about six feet into the fields. There was little talk, but even when sunset brought darkness, no one wanted to leave before the Master. After a time, a pair of bright eyes materialized out of the darkness, steadily approaching the group from behind the Master. At first it was thought to be a cow, but as the animal got closer, it was clear that these were the bright eyes of a big cat. Strangely, no one was able to utter a word or to shout a warning, yet all had a sense that trouble would be averted. The tiger paced up slowly until it was directly behind the Master, then lightly balanced on its hind legs and rested its forepaws on his shoulders. Without moving at all or looking back, as if he had been expecting the animal, Nityananda lifted his right hand and patted the tiger's head. Satisfied, the tiger jumped down and disappeared towards the Mandakini. Later, the Master said tigers are the vehicles of the goddess and since this was the abode of Vajreshwari, tigers were to be expected. In the *Chidakash Gita*, the Master observes that even wild beasts behave like lambs in the presence of *satpurushas* (enlightened beings·

Many tales are told of the Master's ability to understand animals; in Udipi the Master used to tell the owners of a caged parrot that they should release the bird, since it just cursed them all the time. Eventually, Nityananda released the bird himself. On the other hand, in Ganeshpuri during the early forties one devotee always brought his caged parrot for the Master's darshan. In my own experience, during a visit in May of 1944, the Master interpreted the song of a nearby bird: *"He is saying that it will begin to rain in three days."* The bird's weather prediction proved correct. And in yet another instance during the

Ganeshpuri days, he reassured a devotee who was frightened of snakes that the nearby cobra was harmless, since it was chanting.

Among the many distinguished visitors seen in Ganeshpuri was Swami A. of Shirali, who visited in 1951. Swami A. was an enlightened yogi and the ninth guru of a very small but also very advanced community with an enviable record of performance in all spheres of endeavor for the better part of a century. The personification of kindness and humility, the Swami was to some extent dominated by a group of lay advisors. Though as *Mathadipathi* (abbot) his word could be law for the community, he was too mild mannered to exercise that authority. He had been expressing a desire to visit Ganeshpuri since the late forties, but the cabinet which administered the Trust did not wish him to make the trip and the visit was put off on one excuse or another. However, in 1951 he asserted himself and the visit was finally decided upon. The group in the motorcade included Mrs. Muktabai, who has often been quoted in this book, her brother, and his wife. The people in charge of the visit, however, were still not quite reconciled to the event, so they took the Swamiji to Akroli and hurriedly started getting out of the car to take a dip in the kunds. The Swamiji asked if Nityananda was around, to which they replied that he was at Ganeshpuri a couple of miles away. He countered that he thought they had come to see Nityananda and further, he thought that Ganeshpuri also had hot sulphur baths. The leader could not disagree, so the group quietly got back in the cars and proceeded to Ganeshpuri.

The previous day at Ganeshpuri one devotee had stayed overnight. Nityananda told him to heat some cow's milk and set it aside before he left, since a visitor would be coming to the Ashram at about 11 A.M. Swami A. and his party arrived at 11 A.M. They all went to the hot springs. Mrs. Muktabai ran to the Master in his center room saying excitedly, "Deva, our Swamiji has come." He replied, *"Everything is known. Milk has been put aside. Set a chair on the outer veranda of the temple, put a shawl on it, and offer the milk to the Swami."*

The Swamiji had his bath, worshipped at the Bhimeshwar temple, and accepted the milk. The party then entered the Ashram. They crossed in front of the room in which Nityananda was sitting and gathered in the western hall. Still determined to prevent a physical meeting between Nityananda and the Swamiji, members of the group went quietly in pairs to stand before the Master's door and bow. Swami A., on the other hand, was no longer asking about Nityananda. The Swamiji was sitting in the hall saying, "We are experiencing a lot of bliss here and don't feel like getting up." (It is customary for Mathadipathis to refer to themselves in the plural so that the egoistic "I" is avoided.) While the group was pleased that Swami A. was not asking to see Nityananda, nevertheless they worried that the longer they waited, the greater the chances of such a meeting became. They tried to hurry the Swamiji saying, "If we don't leave now we will be late for the evening service." The Swami would reply, "What is there if we are late for the evening service one day? We are in a state of bliss and do not feel like getting up." However, they soon persuaded him to leave; the motorcade left without a physical meeting having taken place.

Mrs. Muktabai stayed behind. She rushed to the Master's room repeating, "Swamiji has left." Nityananda replied *"The meeting took place—the meeting took place. But is that the way? Three persons did not want the meeting to take place."*

It is to be assumed that he had met the Swamiji in a subtle manner, and that was the cause of the Swamiji's state of bliss. In asking if this was the way, Nityananda meant that he could have met the Swamiji anywhere, so there was no need to come to the Ashram. At the same time, he did not wish to embarrass the Swamiji, when his advisors did not want a physical meeting. Quite a number of the Master's devotees belonged to this community and Nityananda had previously told them that Swami A. was a good sanyasi and a true yogi. Apparently to prevent complications, he had blinded the Swamiji's intention to see him for the time being.

When the Swamiji's party was about 10 miles from Ganeshpuri, the Swamiji spoke as if awakening from a reverie: "Oh, we have not met Nityananda!" Immediately the leaders traveling with him said, "Oh, but we have left the place and it is now at least 10 miles away," implying that it was not possible to go there again. To this Swami A. said, "I believe he had come to Shirali once, but we were very young at that time. We were very keen to meet him." Normally, under such circumstances, the persons in charge would have driven back but since they were pleased that the meeting had been avoided, this gentle hint was ignored.

Mrs. Muktabai's brother was very upset by all this subterfuge. He returned to Ganeshpuri the next day and told the Master all that had occurred on the return drive. He added, "I am going to bring the Swamiji again, in view of his keeness to meet you." The Master replied, *"Not necessary. The meeting has taken place. Moreover he is suffering from diabetes and is not very fit; the journey is tiresome. He is a Mathadipathi and has to listen to his people."*

It is not only in the case of Swami A. that Nityananda showed such an acute sensitivity to the true desires and needs of the people before him. Indeed, his extraordinary perceptions were a continuous source of wonder even for those devotees who were very close to him. One devotee, Mr. Mudbhatkal, tells of an instance when the Master saved him from embarrassment. The devotee had a Muslim landlord who was a heart patient and whose activities therefore had to be severely restricted. Since he could not travel to Ganeshpuri, the landlord asked Mudbhatkal to bring him some prasad from Nityananda. When he arrived in Ganeshpuri, the devotee found a number of visitors from Bombay sitting in front of the Master. Mudbhatkal was a shy and sensitive man; he had never asked for prasad for himself and now he was embarrassed to request prasad in front of the visitors. He gave up the idea, even though he felt badly about it. Still fretting a little inwardly, he went before the Master to bow before leaving. As he turned to go, the Master called him back and told him to take a tender coconut. His unspoken desire had been fulfilled.

In a similar vein, a devotee from Santa Cruz tells that as a youngster, he once went to Ganeshpuri along with a small group. One of them was a follower of U. Maharaj, a local saintly person. When the Maharaj heard that his disciple was going to Ganeshpuri, he asked him to take a coconut as his offering to Nityananda. At Ganeshpuri, Nityananda was standing at the gate with his hands resting on the wooden bar, requiring the group to halt a while. The moment he saw them he said, *"Oh yes, the coconut has already been received."* In other words, this thought was as good as the deed. It was like his advising people in the Mangalore days that salutations offered internally reached him and that no physical prostrations and kneeling were needed. In this case, U. Maharaj's thought expressed in Santa Cruz with *shuddha bhavana* (purity of feeling and motive) had already reached him, rendering a physical offering of the coconut unnecessary.

It was also during the early fifties that Shankar Tirth first appeared in Ganeshpuri. Shankar Tirth had wandered as a sanyasi for many years with no peace or contentment until someone told him of Nityananda in Ganeshpuri. He found his answer immediately upon having the darshan of Nityananda. After a couple of days, he asked Nityananda where he should stay. He was told he could occupy the Nath temple, which had been restored by the Master in the mid-thirties. Shankar Tirth went there but appeared shaken the next morning, reporting nightmares of cobras attacking him and telling him to leave. He sought permission to go elsewhere, but was told to return and say that he was staying there at Nityananda's request. He did this, but came back the next morning with the same story. Nityananda insisted that he inform the forces threatening him that he had been sent from Ganeshpuri (i.e., by Nityananda) and all would be quiet. Apparently that settled the issue.

A year or two later, the particular Shankaracharya who had initiated Shankar Tirth was camping at Banaganga and sent word to him to report for final initiation. Shankar Tirth asked Nityananda if this was necessary; when told that it was not, he so informed the Shankaracharya.

A Shankaracharya of Puri also visited Ganeshpuri in the mid-fifties; details of this visit were related to me in a most unusual manner. In 1977, I attended a *harikatha* (scriptural story performed in song and narrative) in Santa Cruz. To illustrate the point that silence could also be eloquent on occasion, the performer told this story:

The Shankaracharya of Puri was spending his *chaturmas* (literally "four months;" it now refers to a time of study) in Bombay. He visited the Dattatreya shrine in Vakola (Santa Cruz East) after the termination of chaturmas. While there, he expressed a desire to visit the Vajreshwari temple; he had written a book on Shakti, and he wanted to visit the goddess's shrine before it was published. Our narrator's services were requisitioned for the purpose and the three of them—the elderly Swami, the *shastri* (title of one learned in the scriptures) and the narrator—motored to Vajreshwari. The Acharya was not very strong, and had to be helped by both his companions on the steps leading to the Vajreshwari shrine. After the visit was over the Shankaracharya for the first time expressed a desire to be taken to Ganeshpuri to see Nityananda. This had not been part of the original itinerary, but they proceeded to Ganeshpuri.

When they arrived, the Master was resting on his narrow bench, with a few people sitting in front of him. The three sat with them. Perfect silence reigned. After some time, the shastri stood up, announced who they were, and said that the Shankaracharya had written a book on Shakti and that they had come for Nityananda's benediction. Silence continued. After a couple of minutes, the Master raised his head and nodded to one of the attendant devotees, who disappeared inside for a moment then reappeared with a mysteriously prepared tray of flowers, fruits, and tender coconuts. He placed the tray before the Shankaracharya and withdrew. Apparently the Master knew the Shankaracharya was coming and had ordered the fruits and flowers to be prepared. But the silence continued. After a few minutes the shastri rose and told the Master that what had transpired in silence was not known to him, but he assumed that the flowers and fruits represented his benediction and that they were accordingly taking leave of him. Saying this and with due salutations all three left the Ashram.

In 1954, G.L. Rao was staying with Swami Shankar Tirth in the Nath Mandir opposite the Vajreshwari temple as directed by the Master. One afternoon Godavarimata from Sakori drove up outside the Vajreshwari temple, and going to Shankar Tirth, asked whether she could be taken to Ganeshpuri. Shankar Tirth asked Rao to accompany Godavarimata. In Ganeshpuri, they found the Master resting in his room with his feet projecting onto the cement platform. Rao announced the arrival of the visitor, who had taken a seat a few feet from the platform. Nityananda replied with a *"Hm."* Rao, who wanted to be hospitable, asked whether he could offer Godivarimata a Coke. The Master agreed. While Rao was getting the beverage, Nityananda arose and sat on the platform. The visiting saint stayed on for two days and later stated that Nityananda had given her the darshan of her own guru. She had come to invite Nityananda to Bombay, to grace a yajna with his presence. The Master replied that he would observe the ceremony from Ganeshpuri. She continued to ask for his physical presence, to which he replied, *"One has to come only if one is not there already."* It is reported that on the final day of the yajna, the saint of Sakori was vouchsafed the darshan of Nityananda.

In 1954 at Vajreshwari Sitarama Shenoy suffered a massive heart attack and immediately succumbed to it. His wife however would not accept this as final; she was determined to take the body to Ganeshpuri. Accordingly, she arranged for a car, bundled the body into it and drove towards the Ashram. While still a quarter of a mile away, the car ground to a halt, and would not start again. The driver told Shenoy's wife that he would not be able to repair the car in the dark, nor would he be able to help her carry the body the remaining distance. Not yet defeated, she left the driver with the body and ran towards the Ashram on foot. She was still about two hundred yards from the Ashram when she heard Nityananda shouting, *"Go back and perform the last rites!"* Although she tried to plead with him, she was ordered away. G.L. Rao was present that evening and he asked the Master why he had not restored Shenoy. The Master replied that if he had, soon no one would go to Chandanwadi (the crematorium in Bombay); every one would come to Ganeshpuri. Rao countered: "But you restored him a few years ago and gave him a fresh lease on life." The Master replied, *"At that time the children were young and perhaps the Divine Force had taken compassion and worked that way. Those conditions do not exist today."*

Thus, while the Master did grant an extension of life in at least this one instance, generally he did not act against inexorable destiny. If pressed, he would arrange a situation in which the individual and destiny could confront one another—as in the story of the congenitally blind little girl told in the *Early Years* section or in the case of the woman advised to bathe her husband in the hot springs and then give him an injection, as will be related in the *Kailas* section. In these "tests," exact compliance was a key factor.

Perhaps the unusual remedies Nityananda sometimes prescribed were such tests. In one instance, a brahmin devotee used to come once a week to read the scriptures before the Master. After a few visits he approached the Master, asking to be cured of his tubercular condition and constant cough. The medicine prescribed was to eat one small frog a day—discarding the head and frying the rest in cow's ghee. The pure vegetarian was horrified, but having sought the cure and received the prescription, he complied with the instructions. His lungs improved, and he developed a taste for frogs in the bargain.

On other occasions Nityananda would direct devotees to follow traditional medical advice without giving any indication that he would intervene in their recovery; thus it would appear that it was the physician who had cured. Indeed, Nityananda never took credit for the cures that occurred as a result of people approaching him. He attributed it to the "Divine Force," saying: *"There is not even the desire to do good to anyone. Everything that happens, happens automatically by the will of God."*

Nityananda was tolerant of the humanity of his followers. He made no demands, issued no commandments, but rather simply asked that people prepare to receive that which he could offer in such abundance. His actions indicate that he felt basic human needs should first be fulfilled and then the heart would be free to turn to God. Many of the stories in this volume reflect the Master's concern for the worldly comfort of his devotees. In the following story, he helps to arrange a marriage.

The prospective (but unaware) groom was an attorney originally from the distant state of Kerala. He was a regular weekend visitor to Ganeshpuri and close to the Master. As the years passed, the devotee felt very keenly the loneliness of his unmarried state and set out to find a wife, although with no immediate success. One day in Ganeshpuri, when the usual crowd had gathered in the old Ashram, the advocate made bold to represent his feelings to the Master. As he finished speaking, the Master pointed to the crowd and said, *"Take one from here."* The prospective groom was nonplussed; he was concerned that perhaps the Master did not like his asking about a private problem and thus gave a casual reply. As he sat and mused, the crowd slowly dispersed, soon leaving only one other man with his wife and daughter. This family had traveled from Kerala to seek Master's aid—they were having difficulty arranging a suitable match for their daughter. Nityananda pointed to his devotee and everything seemed to be settled. The couple's horoscopes were sent to an expert astrologer in Kerala. However, even though several experts were eventually consulted, all pronounced that the horoscopes did not agree and the match should not be arranged. Nityananda was informed of this setback. Although he did not know the horoscopes, he immediately pointed out a particular aspect in the charts which nullified the negative signs correctly read by the Kerala astrologers. When this was relayed to Kerala, the astrologers were in complete agreement; indeed, they were amazed that they had not seen this aspect at once.

Because the Master had such a strong connection with his devotees, he was totally aware of all their feelings; indeed, it appears he felt their suffering. A great devotee from the Mangalore days had such an experience. This woman had never been allowed to handle any money. Indeed, she never sought to handle any, nor had she at any time asked for money from her husband, who was not a very understanding person. However in the mid-fifties after they moved to Bombay, the wife earnestly desired to visit nearby Ganeshpuri, and so did ask her husband for a little money. He demanded to know what she planned to do with it; hearing that she intended to visit Ganeshpuri, he sarcastically said, "And what will be achieved by going there?" After a few seconds, he literally threw a five-rupee note at her. Normally she would not have dreamt of touching money so humiliatingly offered, but since she was determined to go to Ganeshpuri, she picked up the note and went at once.

When she reached the old Ashram a little past noon, she found the devotees restless and the atmosphere tense. The Master had not taken his afternoon meal and as a result the devotees had not eaten either. When approached for instructions about the food, Nityananda had become very upset and brusquely sent the questioner away. The devotees implored the newly arrived woman to try to speak to the Master, since she was familiar with him from the Mangalore days. Accordingly, the woman approached the small room where he was sitting, in the open patio opposite the Krishna temple. Seeing her, the Master relaxed and asked, *"How is he? Has he not changed yet?"* His devotee replied, "Do people change their inborn habits? I have brought some food for you. Shall I bring it along?" He agreed. The incident is recorded to indicate that the Master was very much affected by the humiliating experience inflicted on the devotee some fifty miles away.

Late one evening in 1955, the Master asked his devotee attendants to check how much cash there was in the Krishna temple donation box. When told it was nearly full, he asked that it be cleared, but not emptied; a quarter of the money was to be left. The next morning the box was broken and empty; the money had been stolen. Devotees ran to tell the Master, but he was not surprised. That is why he had ordered the box cleared, he said. Why had some money been left? In the small crowd of devotees the previous evening there had been a poor man praying silently that he wanted to break into the box as he was near starvation. The Master said this had been approved, but the amount of money left in the box was adequate for him for the time being.

Kailas: 1956-1961

In 1956, a new structure was inaugurated at Ganeshpuri. This was the new Ashram, or as it was always called, Kailas. Here the Master lived until just a fortnight before his mahasamadhi in August of 1961. This new building brought with it new procedures as well, since devotee attendants monitored the traffic to Nityananda's private quarters. There were special times set for darshan, and visitors who wished to see the Master at other times had to make arrangements with the devotee attendants.

The Master was sitting on the inner platform in Kailas early one evening in the late fifties. He was sitting in the center of the platform, with the pillows on his extreme left. Through the window in front of him one could see the steps leading to the terrace. A young Swami, head of an important monastery in Udipi, suddenly made an appearance from the entrance to the left of the Master, along with a large number of his followers. Several devotees of the Master were sitting on the ground. One of the followers of the visiting Swami said that the Swamiji needed a seat or in this case a mat or a carpet as he was normally not expected to sit on the bare ground. Nityananda's devotees were somewhat at a loss, since they had not been given any instructions about the visit, and the Master was steadfastly gazing through the window without acknowledging the visitor in any way. The Swami respectfully pushed the pillows towards the wall, and occupied a small portion of the platform. He then addressed the Master in Kanarese. The following conversation took place:

Why do they call you God? (At this the Master looked to his left).
Everyone is a God here including yourself and all the ones who are seated here.
But they call you an incarnation.
Has an incarnate at any time announced that he was one? Has a jnani ever projected himself as one?
Yes, Krishna has, in the *Gita.*
Krishna has not. Only Vyasa has.
But Krishna showed the Vishwaroopa (form of the absolute) to Arjuna as recorded in the *Gita.*
Can Vishwaroopa be seen or shown? [This expression was repeated]. *It is Vyasa Maharshi who wrote it for inculcating faith among the devout.*

The visiting Swami then raised certain points mentioned in the *Gita,* as if to begin a dialectical discussion. He was a *Gita* scholar, as the Master stated after he left. Nityananda, always impatient of dry metaphysical discussion, waved aside the debate: *"What is there in the* Gita? *From beginning to the end, it is advice to renounce, renounce, and renounce—worldliness as well as the desire for fruits. What else is there in the* Gita?" The visiting Swami was considerably moved and withdrew after due salutations. He said that he was happy to have had the Master's darshan. Two of his colleagues were to accompany him but at the last moment they were drawn by some other work. The Master shrugged, saying that when there was yoga, there would be darshan.

A week later, the Master spoke again of this Swami from Udipi, hinting that in his previous incarnation, he had been the priest when the Master was in Udipi. As recorded elsewhere, that elderly Swami had been the only one with some understanding of the stature of the youthful Nityananda; he had issued instructions to all concerned not to harass him. The Master added that past connection had brought the young Swami to Ganeshpuri, and a bright future could be foreseen for him.

On another occasion, one evening some sanyasis came and stood before him as he was resting on the inner platform of Kailas. Nityananda just nodded to them from his sleeping posture and they departed. Some of the devotees present asked who the visitors were; the local devotees were surprised that they had never seen the sanyasis before, since they were very frequent visitors to the Ashram. The Master replied that devotees lived everywhere, not only at Ganeshpuri. He added, *"Some live in the jungles, others in different cities and countries."*

Mrs. Kaikini of Dadar was a faithful follower of a great scholar who could hold an audience spellbound during his brilliant lectures on the translation of the *Gita* by the famous saint Jnaneshwar. She became a regular devotee, every year accompanying the scholar and his followers to Pandarpur on an annual pilgrimage known as Wari. Mrs. Muktabai, who also attended these talks occasionally, became friends with Mrs. Kaikini and in time invited her to Ganeshpuri to meet Nityananda. Mrs. Kaikini demurred, saying that it did not sound like an atmosphere she would enjoy, since she had heard that Nityananda was taciturn, gave no meaningful sermons, and was often harsh or rebuking.

Some time later, just before the annual Wari that year, Mrs. Kaikini missed one of her teacher's regular lectures and instead went to a talk by a rival scholar. This man was a court official who had only recently begun lecturing on Jnaneshwar, but was already building a following. Unfortunately, Mrs. Kaikini's absence was noticed, and when her scholar/teacher heard that she was attending the rival's lecture, he became quite angry and proclaimed that she was not to be allowed to visit his place again, nor could she accompany his group for the Wari from that year onward.

When this message reached Mrs. Kaikini, she was deeply shocked. She had been a faithful follower of the scholar and a member of his Wari group for several years. To be told now that she was to be so severely punished hurt and dismayed her deeply. She could not understand or reconcile what had happened, and friends feared for her mental balance. Mrs. Muktabai again asked if she would like to come to Ganeshpuri; this time, Mrs. Kaikini readily agreed.

Nityananda was sitting on his bench when the party arrived. When Mrs. Muktabai told the Master what had happened, he responded with characteristic brevity, *"Where there is divine wisdom (jnana) can there be difference* (bheda)?" Perhaps the meaning was that if Mrs. Kaikini was listening to the same Jnaneshwar at both places, would it have made any difference if she had listened to it at place A or place B? When told that what worried Mrs. Kaikini most was that she was forbidden to join the Wari group in going to Pandarpur, the Master pointed to the ground before him and shouted, *"This is Pandarpur. No need to go in Wari!"* He repeated this. The authoritative manner in which the Master spoke relieved Mrs. Kaikini immediately and she returned to her home calmed and happy.

The next year, as the time for the Wari again approached, her old instinctive attachment reappeared, and she decided to go to Pandarpur on her own. She had just begun packing when she suddenly became very ill. By the time she had improved enough to travel, the War groups were well on their way to Pandarpur, and she could not attend. The following year was much the same. Again, she started to pack and again she fell ill. It was only then that she realized the validity of the Master's words. From that year on, she no longer felt the strong urge to go to Pandarpur. Several years later when she was seriously ill, she stopped her son from rushing for a doctor by saying, "Don't bother. I can see Nityananda standing there. He has come to take me." A few minutes later she passed away.

Such deathbed visions of the Master were also frequently reported; I was present in one such instance involving Narayan Shetty. Popularly known as Sandow Shetty, he was a familiar figure in Ganeshpuri during the last ten years of the Master's earthly life (1951-1961). He had developed a familiarity with Nityananda and so had some authority in the Ashram; he liked to play the fool with devotees until now and then restrained by the Master. He was a strong man, fond of the fruits that were brought in huge quantities as offerings. Often he would slyly put the best ones aside for himself, after seeking the Master's permission with silent gestures. In response to an objection to this, the Master reproached, *"His desires are simple—let him have them."*

He and I became friendly only a few years before his final illness in 1968. He was hospitalized following surgery; when we went to visit him, he was semi-conscious, and speaking as if to Nityananda: "I hope you remember; you promised me a place. I hope you remember." He passed away a few hours later, though the doctors said he was improving.

Once a well-known singer was staying at Ganeshpuri with a devotee of the Master. The singer was generally considered to be superior in his field but perhaps a little too conscious of his excellence. When he entered the Ashram, there were a few *adivasis* (tribal people) about and the Master was lying on his bench as usual. The mud floor, the adivasis and the Master's apparent indifference all combined to upset the artist; perhaps he felt he would be wasting his talent since the effort would be lost on everyone. He did not sing, but returned to his room. Later that evening a famous singer of the older school arrived and sang for an hour or more before returning to her home. The master singer could hear her and apparently reconsidered his refusal; the next morning he prepared to sing his piece. To his great dismay, he could not perform; somehow his voice simply would not come. He went before the Master to seek permission to sing. The Master said, *"Sing—why not? God has given you the voice—sing his praise. What do you care who listens and who does not?"* Immediately the artist's voice was restored and he burst forth in song. It should be noted that Indian music is a science that is intended to enhance the individual's communion with the Infinite; earning money or winning applause are very incidental features. Most of the songs relate in some manner or other to rebinding the individual to the universal.

A year or two after K.S. Lulla, an attorney devotee, began visiting Ganeshpuri, Nityananda directed him to go to Kanhangad, and then on to Dharmasthal for the darshan of Lord Manjunath before returning. He was asked to travel by air. For the attorney this was the first trip to that part of the country. He first went to Kanhangad, then to Mangalore. From there he planned to motor to Dharmasthal early in the morning before returning to Mangalore to catch his confirmed flight to

Bombay at 11:30 A.M. Accordingly, he arose very early and taxied to Dharmasthal, arriving by 6 A.M. When he tried to enter the shrine for darshan, he was stopped by the priest who told him that darshan was only possible after the ritual worship (*pooja*) was over, near noon. Since the confirmed flight was at 11:30, it was necessary for him to have darshan without much delay. Nonetheless, the priest was firm, saying that according to tradition, even the highest in the land can only have darshan after the pooja. When the devotee persisted in his request, he was taken to the hereditary head of the entire property. This gentleman repeated what the priest had said. Each time he repeated the factual position, the Master's devotee also repeated his plea in the following terms: "Bhagawan had asked me to have darshan. My flight is at 11:30. If it is not possible I will go and I will explain to Bhagawan why I could not have darshan." Intrigued by the repeated expression of "Bhagawan," the head of the property asked to whom reference was being made. When informed that it was to Nityananda of Ganeshpuri, the gentleman immediately asked the priest to take the petitioner privately and allow him to have darshan.

Upon Lulla's return to Ganeshpuri, he was asked what time he had taken darshan of Manjunath, and the questioners gave the exact hour. He was astonished, since this was the correct time, and asked how they had known. The devotees told him that some of them were sitting in front of the Master at that time, and he smiled and said, *"Lulla is having darshan of Manjunath."*

This incident is unusual also because Nityananda generally did not stress participation in rituals or public worship in the traditional sense. He often said, *"gupta bhakti—mukti":* devotion secretly practiced leads to liberation. Bhakti should not be demonstrative. Once, a devotee was known to be speaking of her spiritual experiences to friends in Bombay, implying that she was developing rapidly. On her next visit to Ganeshpuri the Master asked, *"What do you do when you season a dish? After seasoning it, don't you keep it closed for some time?"* Just as a dish is kept covered after seasoning to allow the flavor to permeate the preparation instead of evaporating, similarly spiritual experiences have to be kept to oneself, until one is advanced enough to be able to speak of them without arousing a sense of ego.

The use of a cooking analogy is not so surprising since the Master knew all the finer points of cooking. Sometimes he would give directions on how to grind the masala and what spices should go into it, and so on. When more than one devotee was present at Ganeshpuri, each would prepare a dish, hoping that the Master would accept his offering that day. When the designated devotee would serve Nityananda, the Master could always tell if an ingredient was missing; he would often make suggestions about blending spices or about specifics of preparation. He once told a devotee that as a man became more spiritually evolved, he would be able to cook well instinctively; the ingredients he mixed and blended would go in the right proportion without his having to measure them.

Nityananda's own knowledge of the art of cooking was perfect. G.L. Rao recalls that the Master once prepared an excellent festival dinner for him. When the cooking was completed, Nityananda served Rao the majority of the food, taking only a little for himself on a sheet of newspaper. The Master mixed it with the curry, ate a few morsels while still standing, and then threw away the paper. I also was very fortunate to have enjoyed such an experience with the Master, in 1945. He prepared rice and a potato dish, peculiar to my tribe and my part of the country. He suddenly entered my room with the dish and asked me to eat. I took it a small distance away and began to eat, but to my embarrassment he kept watching me eat. Though it was very tasty, it was a very large portion; when a little was left over and I really could not finish it, he suggested that I might leave it. Some time in 1946 when we were sitting together the Master cryptically told me *"It is good to know cooking."* Though at that time it sounded like a casual utterance with little personal significance for me, a time came over three decades later when I was compelled to learn the elements of cooking for my own sake.

The Master could be very modern in his views. One devotee with a growing family brought his youngest infant to Ganeshpuri for the Master's benediction. It was the devotee's fifth child. There was no one around; the Master gave his blessing and played with the child, but addressed the father: *"Why do you have to produce like the cat family? Go and get operated."*

One evening during 1947 the Master broke the silence to say the following words about Prohibition:

> *What is the use of trying to prevent the poor from drinking? Is it possible to do so? What have you got to offer them in lieu, when the man comes home tired and has not much to feed himself with, but has enough worries of the family like indebtedness, etc.? He has a tot to overcome his tiredness and goes to bed. As it is, every household in this area brews their own liquor from plantains. Drunkenness should be an offense but not drinking, until the people are properly fed and arrangements for healthy recreation exist.*

In the case of a mutton shopkeeper, again Nityananda's view was modern. This merchant had been visiting the Master for some time and had changed his line of business to a general store, perhaps because he thought his hereditary trade of selling meat was unclean. However, his business was very bad and he was losing money. After a few months of continued losses, he sought the Master's benediction. Nityananda's advice was succinct, *"Do your dandha."* Dandha refers to one's normal avocation. In this case, the man reverted to his original trade and started doing well again. The externals do not matter in such cases.

In another instance involving choice of vocation, a young man who was the son of devotee parents and who was himself very attached to the Master came to Ganeshpuri with a problem. He wanted very much to become a pilot but his parents did not approve. The boy appealed to the Master who approved his choice. To the parents Nityananda said, *"What danger is there? Cannot an accident occur on the roads? Let him go."* Unfortunately the boy could not pass the eye test; a serious condition was detected which could lead to total blindness. The boy went to the Master, who gave him a little bottle of oil to be used regularly—on the scalp. Three months later he was declared fit in a new eye test. Many years later, he discussed this situation with some eye specialists who confirmed that the originally diagnosed condition inevitably causes loss of sight.

The Master attracted many people to Kailas in Ganeshpuri, including other spiritual teachers and leaders. The extraordinary visit by Swami A. has already been recounted. Perhaps one of the most fruitful of these visits was made by Swami Chinmayananda. Mr. Suvarna recalls one of the earliest visits; it was a bright afternoon at the Kailas Ashram. Mr. Suvarna, serving as doorkeeper, opened the door to find that Swami Chinmayananda and Dr. Nair had come for the darshan of Nityananda. Suvarna announced the visitors to the Master and welcomed them in. The exact year of this visit is not known but it was between 1956 and 1959. As a result of his visits, the Swami often spoke of Nityananda during his talks, referring to him as the living *stithaprajna* (one who is always the witness; the highest spiritual attainment) of the *Gita*. Some time in 1960, he announced a spiritual picnic for his disciples to take place in Ganeshpuri. The Master received the Swami and his many followers with band music and all the honors due a visiting religious dignitary. Following these greetings, Swami Chinmayananda was invited to give a talk to the assembled devotees from the terrace of the newly opened Bangalorewalla building.

The Master was kind to him and said that since he had *Saraswati shakti* (Saraswati, goddess of widsom; shakti, power) he might utilize it to spread the message of the *Upanishads*. Swami Chinmayananda considered himself blessed by the Master, and always referred to him in the highest terms. He said that compared to Nityananda we were mere infants in the spiritual sense: "To repeat the actual experiences of his devotees, the strange methods the yogi evolved, the seemingly mad acts he did, would read [like] a saga of a hundred Christs living together, each exhibiting his wonderous powers in ameliorating the sufferings of the poor."

But as long as the Master remained in his human form, the weak-nesses of the flesh remained also. By 1957, the Master's teeth were de-teriorating; although this did not seem to be causing him any difficulty, two devotees who spent much time in Ganeshpuri urged him to have his teeth removed, threatening to fast if he did not agree. The Master ul-timately agreed to having the teeth extracted, but would not agree to the normal anesthetic (cocaine) injection. Thus, there was conside-able pain and bleeding. Soon after the extractions, the two devotees of-fered the Master a meal to eat, even though he was still bleeding. He refused, saying to the other devotees, *"How can a meal be eaten when the teeth have just been removed? Yogis also suffer from pain but their attention is never linked to it and so they don't seem to feel it."*

For devotees, the relationship between physical manifestations and spiritual truth has always been a difficult area. For the Master, it was sublimely simple. In the late fifties, some devotees complained to Nityananda that old age and distance prevented them from visiting him more often. His response was, "Samadhan *(mental equilibrium) wher-ever you are situated."* In other words, he was again confirming that his grace was available even without his physical presence. As he used to say to his devotees in the early days in South Kanara, *"Wherever de-votees meet and talk [about him], this one is there."* To others from Ka-nara, who complained that the devotees in Bombay were lucky as they could see him any time they liked, whereas they could not afford to come often, he said, *"The fish are born, grow and die in the Ganges. Do they attain liberation as a result?"* Physical proximity is not the criterion for the miracles of samadhan and liberation.

The talk then turned to seva. Someone asked what would be the re-sult of performing seva for satpurushas. In a rather angry tone, the Mas-ter replied, *"Who wants seva? Does the God ask to be worshipped? It is the man who does so, to get something out of him. Go back and do your duty without desire for fruit, and without sacrificing efficiency. That is the highest seva that you can render. As for spiritual progress, the essential thing is* vairagya *[intense sense of renunciation and dispas-sion for worldliness]. Without such vairagya there can be no progress whatsoever, and if you don't listen you will fail in the end."*

On another occasion, a devotee found that both of the Master's feet were considerably swollen, and asked him what the matter was. He told her, *"All people come here for seva. They also deposit their desires and difficulties at the feet and while the ocean of divine mercy washes away much of the effect, a little has to be accepted by the body, which has been assumed only for the sake of the devotees."*

The Master did much for the sake of the devotees; in this story from 1959, the pleas of an old Gujarati devotee and his wife led Nityananda again to offering relief while leaving some elements to fate. It was during the monsoon of 1959. A long line of devotees and petitioners were waiting outside Kailas for their turn to be admitted. The wife of the Gujarati devotee was fourth in the line, but she pleaded with Mr. Suvarna (who was serving as doorkeeper) to be allowed inside. As he was about to open the door, the Master shouted at him from inside on the cement platform that he was not to open the door. Suvarna immediately withdrew, but the woman continued to plead with him through the window. Nityananda also continued shouting that the doors were not to be opened. Suvarna was becoming quite embarrassed as he was caught between the pleas of the devotee and the shouted commands of the Master. Finally, knowing that the woman was a good devotee, he took the liberty of opening the door despite the shouts from the Master. As soon as the next four people were admitted, he was about to close the door behind the pleading woman but she further begged him not to close the door yet, since it was for the sake of her ailing husband that she was persevering, and he was further down the line. He had been very ill for some time, and Nityananda was their last hope. Suvarna was moved by her pleas, especially since it was drizzling, so out of sheer pity he chose to disregard the warning shouts given by the Master and let them all in, even though he feared he might be taken to task later on for doing so. (He was not.) The woman waited while the devotees had their darshan, then she pleaded with the Master to cure her husband. He was silent for some time, then said, *"Give him a bath in the kunds and later an injection."* As soon as she heard the words of the Master, she knew her husband would be saved. She left happily, and was taking her husband to the hot springs when she saw the dispensary on their way as they turned the corner. She stopped there first, had her husband injected, and went on to the kunds. But as they entered the hot water, the man passed away and was pulled out dead.

It can be postulated that the man had already died when the wife wanted the doors to be opened, hence the Master's shouts against opening them. However, after they were opened and as a result of the wife's pleadings, the Master allowed destiny and their own good sense to decide the issue. Hence though the woman was told that her husband should be bathed in the kunds and then given an injection, she had him injected first and then taken to the kunds. On all occasions, but particularly in cases like these, the instructions received are very important and have to be complied with to the letter. This was conveyed to the woman later by other devotees who were present when the instructions were given to her.

Dr. Cooper was given the secret for preparing a drug with wide-spectrum curative properties by a Himalayan saint in the early twenties. The doctor had just returned from studies in England. He was brought to Ganeshpuri in 1959 by the late Dr. Deodhar. Dr. Cooper had heard of Nityananda and wanted to speak with him about the future of this drug. The doctor was accommodated in the neighboring sanatorium, and after refreshing himself was taken to Kailas by Dr. Deodhar and some others. The Master was sitting in the first room to the left. As they stood before him, no words were spoken. Dr. Cooper remained gazing silently at the Master; streams of tears coursed down his face. After a time, his friends took him away to a restaurant. As they drank their tea, Dr. Deodhar reminded Dr. Cooper that he had come to discuss the medicine with Nityananda, yet they had not spoken at all; only tears had come from the doctor. To this the visitor could only shake his head: "You come here so often; apparently you see only his outer form. I saw a dazzling crystal in his head. It made me tongue-tied. As for the tears I do not know. I was overcome with emotion at his purity and felt an acute awareness of the separation that I had suffered from the Divine. It was this split-second sense of reunion that caused the tears." A detailed account of the drug which Dr. Cooper bequeathed to the Nityananda Hospital before he passed away is given in Appendix C.

As Dr. Cooper noted, frequent visitors to Ganeshpuri were in danger of limiting their vision to only the physical aspect of the Master. For one with this orientation, Nityananda's physical form raised many perplexing questions. Already by the early 1940s, he was somewhat heavier than during the Mangalore-Kanhangad days. By 1944-47, he was clearly putting on weight, yet there was no organized kitchen in Ganeshpuri until the early fifties. Before that, even though devotees who stayed on for several days did cook their meals there, and of course offered this food to the Master, he did not always partake of it. Thus, there were no regular cooking arrangements until the western room of the old Ashram was converted into a simple kitchen in the early fifties. Restaurants and other sources of food also began to open in the area of the Ashram in the early fifties. Thus the Master's intake was irregular and certainly well below that of an average person.

By 1959-60, the Master had assumed outsize proportions and by the end of 1960 his waistline was very large. However, his eating habits had in no way changed; if anything, solid food was no longer taken as he had not agreed to wearing a false set of teeth. Noting these changes in his physical form, four devotees individually and on different occasions voiced their concern for his growing waistline. Sandow Shetty was one of the first to raise this question. As at one time he had been fond of gymnastics and feats of strength, the Master told him that the present increase in his weight was due to lack of exercise. Mr. G.L. Rao in his turn raised this same question. It may be recalled that Rao was a chronic malaria patient. The Master told him that he also used to be a victim of malaria and that the size of his waistline was due to an enlargement of the spleen. Another devotee who practiced regular pranayama exercises, was told that the size of the stomach was due to breath retention. To Mrs. Muktabai who came to him in concern for his health and comfort, the Master said that the love of all devotees had come and settled down in that area and thus the great size. Whatever the true cause of the changes in the Master's physical proportions, it is likely to have had nothing to do with the intake of food. By the time he attained mahasamadhi in August 1961, the Master was again reduced to thinness.

The feeding of the poor, however, was a frequent and regular feature. Food brought as an offering by devotees was distributed among the local poor children. In later years with the increasing crowds of devotees, the number of fruit baskets and flowers used to pile up. While some would be distributed, others would be allowed to rot and then ordered to be buried. Once Sandow Shetty ventured to ask the Master why he was allowing the fruits to go to waste. He was told, *"They are not going to waste. Those for whom they are meant are consuming it."*

Three years before his mahasamadhi, in 1958, Nityananda directed that a feeding of poor children (*bal bhojan*) be instituted in Ganeshpuri on a permanent basis. This was done; by 1961, a little over a hundred of the local poor children were fed one meal every morning. Today over 700 children are provided with one free meal at about 10 o'clock in the morning. In addition, there are three or four public feedings a month, when nearly 2500 poor adivasis of all ages are fed. Although no funds are actively collected for this purpose, the bal bhojan account is always overflowing, with unsolicited donations coming from all quarters. In the late fifties, similar programs were started at the Kanhangad Ashram. Today every one of the Ashrams built in his name feeds the local poor at least once a day, to the extent of the funds available. It will be noticed that in the Nadigrantha reading in the Appendix it is said that Nityananda was fond of feeding and that the goddess Annapoorna was behind him. This seems to be borne out in every one of the Ashrams being run in his name.

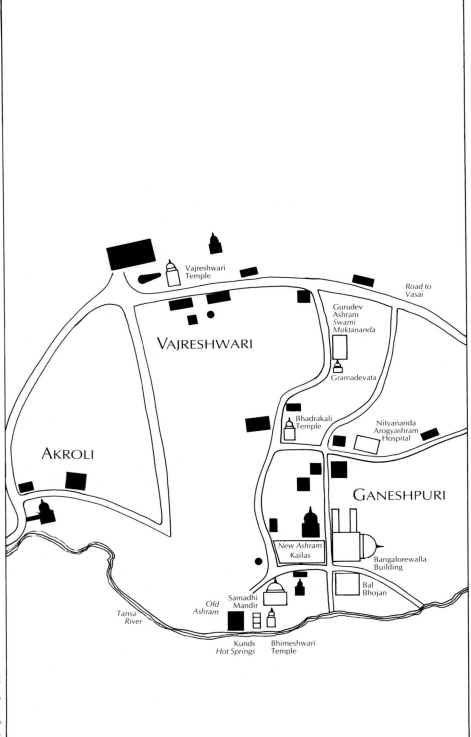

Vajreshwari
Temple

Road to
Vasai

Gurudev
Ashram
*Swami
Muktananda*

VAJRESHWARI

Gramadevata

Bhadrakali
Temple

Nityananda
Arogyashram
Hospital

AKROLI

GANESHPURI

New Ashram
Kailas

Bangalorewalla
Building

Bal
Bhojan

*Tansa
River*

*Old
Ashram*

Samadhi
Mandir

Kunds
Hot Springs

Bhimeshwari
Temple

Shrines in Ganeshpuri

Nityananda often said that Ganeshpuri was a holy place from ancient times. He would sometimes speak of the past glory of the area, recounting important Puranic incidents, or describing the eruption of Mandakini. In keeping with this history, Ganeshpuri has many shrines, several constructed at the Master's instruction.

Bhimeshwar Temple: There are several stories relating to this ancient shrine near the Master's ashram. Dr. Deodhar remembers that some time around 1950 he noticed that the silver cobra *(Naag)* was missing from the linga in the temple. He intended to consult Nityananda about this, but it kept slipping his mind during his visits, only to be remembered when he was halfway home. This continued for some time. Finally, when he once again realized that he had still not sought the Master's instructions, he decided to send another devotee for the Master's orders. When this devotee arrived, the Master said, *"You have come for that? He always forgets! Tell him he has the approval to have the Naag made, but it should be in copper."* He then gave detailed instructions on the exact size, how the body should be, the eyes, the mouth, and so on. He directed the devotee to measure the size with a thread, according to the instructions given. He then said that it should be installed on the following Monday—that was four days away. This very short preparation time caused the doctor some anxiety; he didn't know where to go or what to do next. He went to the market and contacted various artisans, but no one would do it in copper; they said it would ruin their families. Finally he was told that there was only one person in the entire district who would make it in copper; after contacting this smith and confirming that he could manufacture the Naag according to the instructions given, the doctor was told the process would take at least 10 days. Deodhar's face fell; when he explained that the statue was needed for installation on Monday, the smith agreed to call in all his workers and be ready in time.

When the doctor arrived to pick up the Naag, he found that the eyes were not shining as instructed. The smith said he had not put any beads in because they would fall off and the cavities would be unsightly. Just then a Shiva statue was brought in; its eyes were brightly painted. It was agreed to give the snake the same treatment.

On seeing the Naag, the Master was satisfied and asked that it be kept on a shelf in front of him until the installation, which took place with due ceremony the next morning.

Another most unusual feature of the Bhimeshwar temple was the continuous dripping of water from the ceiling at the rear of the dome. Some time in the early forties, after Nityananda made Ganeshpuri his permanent abode, water started dripping from a number of points on the ceiling and falling behind the main linga. This water increased both in quantity and speed—by the mid-forties one could collect a spoonful of water in seconds, even in the height of summer. My uncle pointed this out to me and also told me that the Master had cautioned him not to tread on the small lingas that were springing up where the water fell. Two well shaped linga-like projections had developed immediately behind the main linga in two holes that were always filled with water. The others were projections of various shapes in a rough semi-circle behind the linga. The Master would occasionally refer to this phenomenon, saying that scientists would come and hold a torch and see how the water fell; without saying anything more, he would laugh heartily.

There are some who explain these automatic lingas as stalactites. I would ask, however, where these stalactites were hiding before the Master's arrival. Also, where did they go after the Master's mahasamadhi? For as soon as he left the old Ashram for Kailas in 1956, the water flow slowed to the merest trickle. The remaining small flow continued to diminish after the mahasamadhi, but most surprisingly, stopped completely the day the Master's statue was installed in the Samadhi Mandir temple.

Gramadevata: One day in 1945, on a monthly weekend visit, I suddenly noticed a small shrine within 200 yards of the road leading to the ashram. This is where Swami Muktananda's Gurudeva Ashram is situated at present. When I reached the Ashram that day in 1945, the Master told me that the shrine was the *gramadevata* (grama, village; deva, god) established by him. Later he is quoted as saying, *"There is the force of a samadhi there, and the place has to develop."*

Krishna Shrine: Prior to the construction of this shrine, the relic of an old stone *Nandi* (name of the bull that is Shiva's vehicle) lay in its place. How it came to be there is not known. I remember occasionally seeing the Master sit on it with both his feet on its left side. The Nandi had to be removed when the Krishna shrine was being constructed. Although a large number of people tried to lift the stone, it would not budge. They brought the problem before Nityananda, who asked for a coconut to be broken near it. After this was done, two people could easily lift the great stone. Nityananda had the head of this Nandi cut to provide a head for the cow behind the Krishna statue.

Bhadrakali Shrine: Shortly after the Krishna shrine was completed, the Master arranged to construct the Bhadrakali shrine. Whenever Nityananda decided to construct such shrines, very little time was wasted; he would set a specific day for inauguration and all work would have to be completed by that time. B. Mistry was given one day to prepare the statue. He used the same cement mixture as he had used earlier for the Krishna statue, as ordered by the Master. When everything was ready, and the statue had been made within a day, the priest anxiously informed the Master that the face of the goddess looked anything but attractive! The Master reassured him that all would be well and ordered the statue covered with a white cloth till the next morning when the consecration was to take place. The next day when the cloth was removed, the statue displayed a face attractive enough to satisfy even the priest's aesthetic expectations.

When asked about the urgency in getting this temple ready, the Master informed the devotees that Bhadra Kali had followed him from Gokarn and wanted a place in Ganeshpuri. She was not prepared to wait any longer.

In addition to shrines commissioned by the Master, several beautiful shrines were dedicated to Nityananda after his mahasamadhi. The first temple constructed on the Kanhangad rock was opened in April 1963 ﹍nd the one in Guruvana in May 1966. The Rock Temple was constructed by Mr. B.H. Mehta from funds he collected; it was designed by the same architect as the Guruvana temple and the actual Samadhi Mandir at Ganeshpuri. If the Kanhangad rock can be compared to the brain as the Master indicated, then it is very appropriate that Nityananda should be at the top and center of the Brahmarandra!

The Samadhi Mandir: The imposing Samadhi Mandir was designed by Mr. Prabhashankar Sompura, architect of the well known Somnath Temple and also designer of the two temples dedicated to the Master in Kanhangad. The Samadhi Mandir is located on the site of the original Ashram of the Master, and is where his holy remains lie interred. The Samadhi Mandir and the hall constitute an imposing edifice, with the 24 foot high dome giving the temple a total height of over 100 feet. The Tansa river flowing a little distance away adds to the tranquil beauty of this holy site.

Many other temples have been dedicated to Nityananda by his devotees, householder and sanyasi alike. These holy shrines range from small altars simply adorned with a photograph to elaborately beautiful constructions such as the fine temple with a large hall constructed by Mr. M.L. Gupta in Koilandi near Calicut, scene of the young Ram's activities during his years with Mr. Ishwar Iyer.

Swami Janananda at the Kanghangad Ashram.

Nityananda wished to have sunrise-sunset caves hewn from the rock.

It was here that Nityananda struck a rock and brought out clear spring water, which has been flowing ever since. It is called Papanashini Ganga.

Viakunt—the old Ashram.

Bhimeshwar temple (interior and exterior).

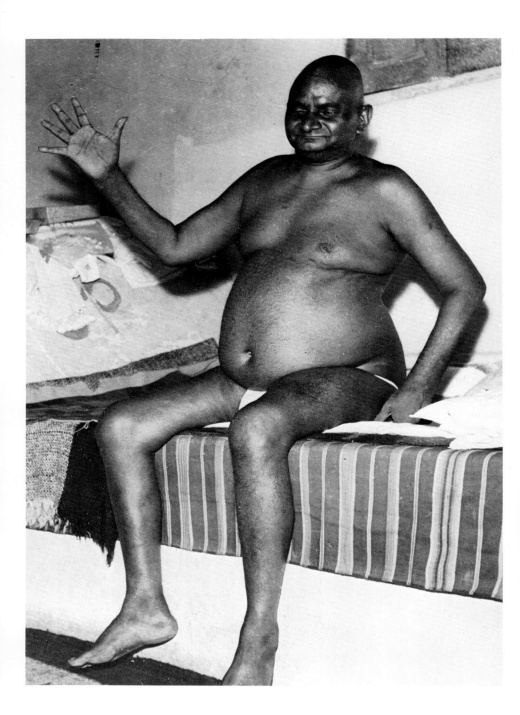

Nityananda and His Photographer

Nityananda greatly resisted being photographed during his early years; very few pictures from that period are known. In contrast, after the arrival of Mr. Suvarna as described below, many fine photographs of the Master became available. The section that follows reproduces all the early photographs known to the publisher. In addition, Mr. Suvarna has given generously from his unique file of photographs; many of these are here published for the first time.

One of the earliest photographs in this section appears to have been taken in Mangalore prior to the twenties. It shows Nityananda seated and in deep concentration. The young Master looked like this when I first saw him in Mangalore, in about 1920. Another photograph was taken in about 1924, in the compound where Mrs. Krishnabai lived. In those days, the photographer had to make many slow and painstaking adjustments in order to focus properly. Nityananda's devotees were not sure he would be willing to sit for the time needed for this undertaking. Some of the women had woven a garland for him, but he threw it away immediately. Since the cameraman was still not ready, the devotees hurriedly prepared another with whatever flowers, leaves, and stems were readily available, and put it on him just as the cameraman clicked. This is the photo that shows him with a garland. Two other photos from this same time period may in fact be part of this series. Although they are of poor quality (perhaps taken as a test of camera settings), they are nonetheless interesting since they show the deep

concentration of the young Master and his disregard for the surroundings. In the photo showing him pulling apart the garland, his attention
is clearly focused within. Devotees often asked to have a photograph
of Nityananda taken with their families. Two of these, both taken in
about 1927, are shown; in one the young Nityananda is sitting with Mr.
Shenoy's family in Bombay; in the other he holds Mrs. Muktabai's
eldest son.

However, the young Nityananda normally discouraged people from
revering his photographs and actually admonished them for doing so.
Once Mrs. Krishnabai felt that since he had obliged the photographer
in her own compound, she might be permitted to keep his picture in
her house. Accordingly, she arranged for the photographer to send a
special copy of the Master's portrait to her mother's house to be collected in a couple of days. When Mrs. Krishnabai went to her mother's
house to collect the framed photograph, it was evening. Electricity had
not come to Mangalore yet, and only a few kerosene lamps were burning; she did not notice the Master who was sitting in a dark corner. As
she was asking her mother about the photograph the Master burst out,
*"You want to keep a photograph, do you? Go to the dung heap—your
photograph is lying there."* She went to the dung heap and looked for
it, but was told by her mother that the Master had taken a stone and
powdered the framed picture.

Photographs of Nityananda became readily available only after Mr.
M.D. Suvarna of Foto Corner at Khar, Bombay 52, arrived in
Ganeshpuri in the early fifties. Originally a press photographer,
Suvarna and his colleague had learned of Nityananda's growing popu-
larity and realized that there would soon be a demand for good photographs of the Master. They decided to go to Ganeshpuri. Nityananda
shouted and thundered at the photographers, who retreated in haste.
However, Mr. Suvarna decided to take one more chance and his per-
sistance was rewarded. Permission was granted, although not until
after considerable pleading. In addition, there were riders attached to
the approval: there was to be no disturbance, no fuss, and no posing.

Although Suvarna had gone to Ganeshpuri simply as a photographer, he remained to become a sincere devotee. Whenever he was
in Bombay he made it a point to be in Ganeshpuri every Thursday and
to expose one roll of film during each such visit. The photographs have

come out so well that many of them could be mistaken for posed portraits. Thus, Suvarna's arrival at Ganeshpuri changed the almost never photographed Nityananda into one of India's most photographed saints.

There is considerable variance in detail from picture to picture. This was pointed out to me by Mr. Wagh, the well-known sculptor, who was using the photographs as aids in preparing the statue for the altar in the Samadhi Mandir. However the photographs consistently portray mystic power, compassion, and blissful relaxation.

Some time in the late fifties, Mr. Suvarna exposed a few hundred feet of motion picture film taken at odd moments and spliced them together. Much to his surprise, since it was the first time he had handled a film camera, the pictures came out very well. On the other hand, there were occasions when he was equally surprised to draw a blank. For instance, once he wanted to photograph the Master as he returned from his morning walk. After arranging for a hole to be bored in the wall of a nearby hotel, Suvarna waited at his pre-adjusted camera and took several shots of the Master passing by, but no picture developed. When he repeated the experiment, there was the same result. The Master would sometimes ask him, *"What is the value of so many pictures? Are you still not satisfied?"* But when Suvarna persevered, Nityananda only smiled.

On one other important occasion Suvarna's cameras unaccountably would not function. He and his cousin failed to get a single picture of the Master's body on August 10, 1961, two days after the mahasamadhi, when the holy remains were in the process of being interred. First, the body was placed in his easy chair and then mounted on a jeep, to be slowly driven around the buildings in Ganeshpuri. Mr. Suvarna was able to film this last journey and took several good pictures despite the steady drizzle. However, when the body was taken to the old Ashram for interment, even though he and his cousin stood at two different vantage points and each exposed a full roll of film during the ceremonial interment, they were astonished to find that not one of the 24 frames exposed had caught even a single image.

The
Photographs

The devotees hurriedly prepared another with whatever was readily available—this is the photo that shows him with a garland.

We must visualize the Nityananda of those days: looking like an eccentric vagrant, his body wire-thin as if lashed by severe austerities, but healthy and glowing all the same.

    The Master was a regular visitor at Mrs. Muktabai's home in Bombay. Once the Master managed the house, attending to all the household chores himself.

    It was a bright morning. The youthful Master was, as usual, walking at his faster-than-wind pace.

The sculptor of the statue for the Samadhi Mandir pointed out there is considerable variance in detail from picture to picture.

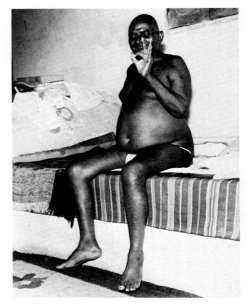

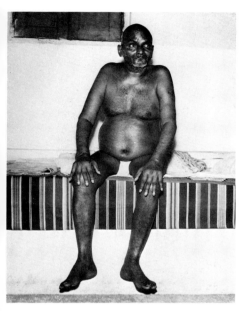
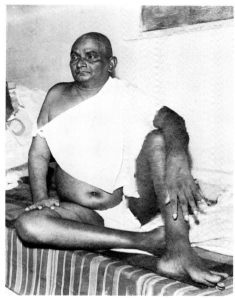
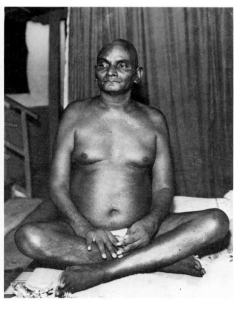
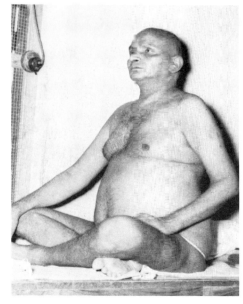

"Once one is established in infinite consciousness, one becomes silent and though knowing everything, goes about as if he does not know anything."

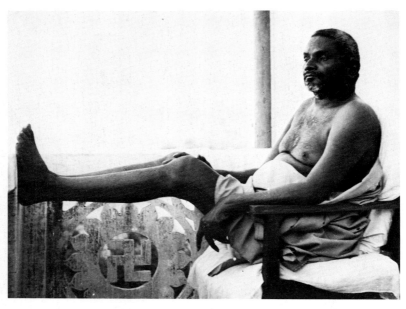

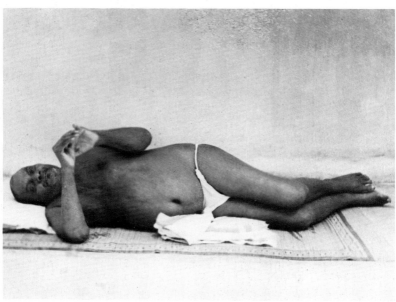

"To be able to forget everthing and be aloof, that alone is the highest state to be in."

"Though he might be doing a lot of things in several places, to all outward appearance, he will remain as if he does nothing."

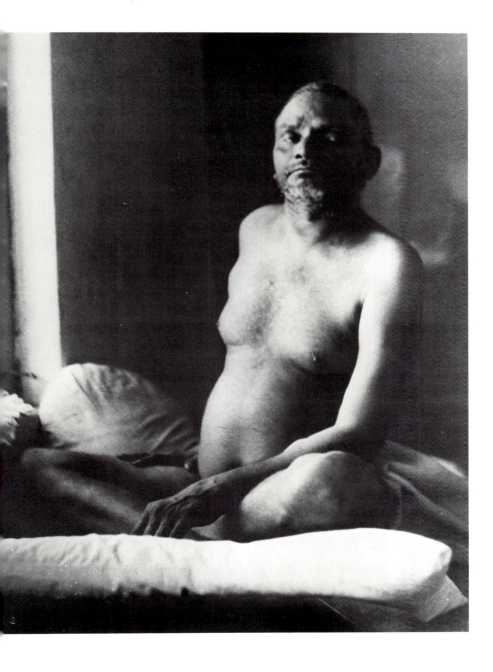

"No going anywhere in future; here only."
(Photographs taken in Kailas.)

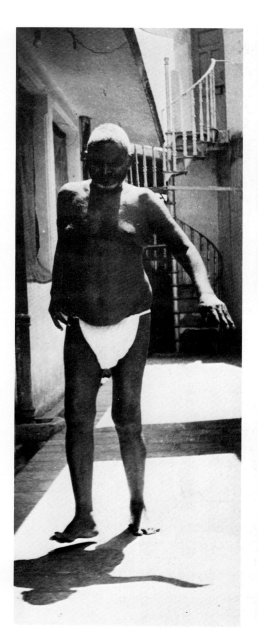

"He will always remain as if he is a witness to everything that goes on, like a spectator at a cinema show, and not be affected by the pleasant or the unpleasant."

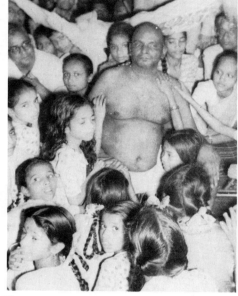

"With his index finger pointing to the spot I occupied in the old Ashram, he replied, "*That alone is good.*"

Swami Chinmayananda and Nityananda.

"*There are so many things in this Ashram. If this one goes elsewhere, none of these things would be taken.*"

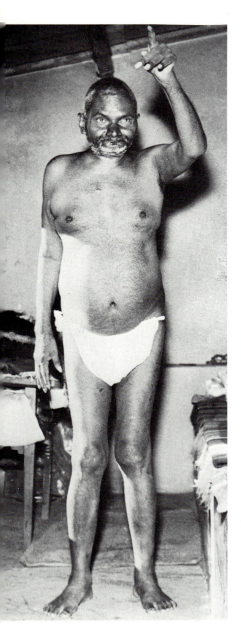

His photographs consistently portray mystical power, compassion, and blissful relaxation.

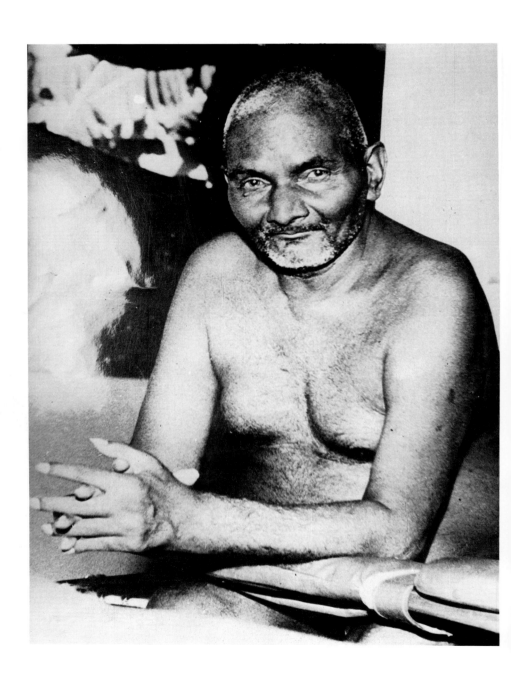

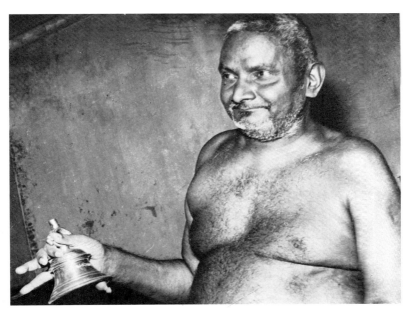

On July 27, 1961, his last Guru Purnima day, he addressed the assembled devotees. He spoke for nearly 45 minutes in his normal tone, even though he was very weak.

On August 8, 1961, [Nityananda] attained mahasamadhi in the main hall of the Bangalorewalla Building. The area is now treated as a sanctified place with regular daily rituals performed at the times of worship.

The Mahasamadhi

August 8, 1961

The following account of the last months and days is really a patchwork of the reminiscences of many devotees. My personal knowledge of these events is limited to my sense of foreknowledge in the last several months and then to my final trip to Ganeshpuri to pay my respects to the earthly remains of the Master. In between, the account of Nityananda's departure from the physical form is woven of many strands. Those sections being narrated directly by me are given in the first person.

◇ ◇ ◇

On the afternoon of July 25, 1961, Nityananda asked for a chair to be brought to Kailas as he wished to move to the Bangalorewalla building. He was too weak to walk that distance. He told Gopalmama that he was going to the Bangalorewalla building for only a fortnight. Exactly one fortnight later, on August 8, 1961, he attained mahasamadhi in the main hall of the Bangalorewalla building. His bed has not been moved; the area is now treated as a sanctified place with regular daily rituals performed at the times of worship.

The months just prior to the mahasamadhi were filled both with portents of the Master's leaving his physical body and with signs easily misread by devotees reluctant to accept his imminent passing. Much confusion was engendered by the ongoing discussions and plans concerning a move to the city of Bangalore. This plan was primarily fostered by Mr. Lakshmansa Khoday, a sincere devotee who had been responsible for the construction of the Bangalorewalla building. Khoday had gone so far as to charter a plane for moving the Master.

Devotees hearing of this proposed move rushed to Ganeshpuri, many to argue against the idea, since it would leave the Master less accessible to them. Nityananda's answer to these concerns was that he had no intention of moving and that it was the suggestion in *"the assembly of sages"* that *"it be here only."* However, no one understood the implication of the expression "it be here only"; only in retrospect was it understood. Thus, plans continued for the proposed move; it was not until the day prior to the scheduled departure for Bangalore that the Master developed diarrhea and the air trip was cancelled.

The advantage of clear hindsight, however, allows one to see many signs of the impending departure from human form, particularly in the last three months. The move to the Bangalorewalla building itself could be seen thus, since it is the only building in Ganeshpuri large enough to allow easy entry, movement, and exit for the large numbers of devotees who came for the last darshan of the body. Also, some thought the Master had chosen to give up the human body in this place as a token to the faithful devotee Khoday who had constructed the building and who had been disappointed in his wish to transport the Master to Bangalore.

The Master's concern about the reconstruction of the old Ashram can also be viewed in this light. Some time in early June, he inquired whether the devotees who had promised to have the old Ashram rebuilt had done so. He was informed that the old Ashram had been razed and the new walls were up but they had not yet been covered. It was planned to postpone placing the roof slab until after the monsoon season which was about to begin. The Master however insisted that there was no time to waste: the slab should be put on immediately, using Ashram funds if necessary. This was done and the roof went up before the outbreak of the monsoon. It was in this rebuilt section of the Viakunt (old) Ashram that the Master's earthly remains were interred; this would not have been possible if the roof slab had not been set.

Mrs. Muktabai recalled a conversation with the Master shortly after he had moved to the Bangalorewalla building that took on quite different significance later. The Master told her there would be a big yatra (pilgrimage) to Ganeshpuri in a fortnight's time, and that a lot of people would attend. Mrs. Muktabai told me later that as she heard these words, it never occurred to her to ask what pilgrimage there could be during the monsoon.

Of the many signs vouchsafed to devotees in these last months, most were thus misinterpreted or ignored—indeed it was as Swami Yogananda said, when satpurushas reveal something about the future, the listener is prevented from questioning. One devotee who did not misread the signs was a woman devotee from Dadar, called Mataji by her followers and Mantrasiddhibai by the Master. She came to Ganeshpuri for a visit during May of 1961. The day before she arrived, the Master had developed a discharge from his ear. He did not complain of any pain, nor was there any odor to the discharge. The devotees called in a respected ENT specialist who, though he had never seen the Master before, prostrated himself and refused to prescribe any medication until the Master gave his categorical assurance that he would recover. After the Master nodded his assent, the doctor gave some capsules to the attendant devotees along with instructions for their administration. After the doctor left, Gopalmama offered the Master a capsule. He took it, saying that since the doctor had given them with such bhavana, one might be taken. When later offered a second dose, he said, *"One is enough, his bhavana has worked."* And indeed, the discharge had stopped.

As soon as she learned of the discharge, Mantrasiddhibai began to cry and beg the Master not to go away. She interpreted this to be a sign that the Master was cleansing his system of toxins and that only for one purpose. The Master told her, *"Why are you crying? Don't cry. More work is possible in the subtle than in the gross."* This assurance was given to other devotees as well, although they did not interpret the remark as referring to the Master's passing. To Mrs. Muktabai the Master said the ear had sustained some interior damage as a result of a serious injury caused by a fall while he was in the Kanheri caves (1938 or '39). It would therefore appear that the system was being cleansed of impurities of long standing.

Dr. Pandlaskar, a devotee and regular monthly visitor to Ganeshpuri, first heard of the mahasamadhi in a most unusual manner. On the morning of the day Nityananda attained mahasamadhi, the doctor's young son (then nine years old) arose very early and immediately confronted his parents, speaking in a very authoritative tone: "What are you doing here? Go to Ganeshpuri. He will be going today. There is a call for him from the assembly of the sages for help he alone can render, in connection with the forthcoming ashtagraha yoga [13] which portends great evil to the world in general and to India in particular." The parents were so surprised at the boy's unseemly tone and manner that they ignored his words and simply rebuked him.

That evening they received word of the mahasamadhi and traveled at once to Ganeshpuri. The boy was affected by the experience and was not fully normal again for some years.

---

[13] This refers to the conjunction of eight planets in one sign. The next occurrence of this phenomenon would have been in February of 1962, when the planets would be in Capricorn, the sign of India. The boy, of course, had no knowledge of astrology or its interpretation.

It was a hot May afternoon in 1961 when I first heard the telepathic bell announcing that Nityananda would soon be discarding his human frame. My first fear was that he had already done so. I resisted the thought as much as I could, but was not very successful. The next morning I opened the paper with some reluctance, even though it would have been unlikely for the Delhi editions to devote any space to such an unpolitical event in Bombay. I was relieved all the same not to find any mention in the obituary columns, but the mental suggestion that he would be going remained with me, off and on, for the next three months.

The prospect of his going away was frightening to me. Suddenly I was afraid that I had not carried out any real spiritual practices. It is true that the Master had once ruled out the necessity of even having to read anything but now that this idea of his going was overpowering me, I felt very inadequate. I did not feel strong enough to face the prospect of not being able to contact him in the physical form. At that time I had not heard of his assurance that *"more is possible in the subtle."* It is also true that I had received some training in maintaining a relationship with him without frequent physical meetings, since after 1948 my visits were infrequent and largely public; I no longer had the privilege of private time in his company as I had had prior to 1948. He once said that when the child learns to walk and play, the mother must allow it freedom to move and run about, even while keeping a watch on its activities. Perhaps he should have added, "even if the child tries to hang on to the mother!" Of course, there were many indications that his grace was with me wherever I was stationed; but I had also always known that he could be physically contacted if necessary.

Unable to leave the station for a variety of reasons, I thought of a plan to relieve my anxiety. Mrs. Muktabai was a regular visitor to Ganeshpuri, going at least once every fortnight. I wrote to her requesting that she send me a report of the Master's health on each visit, and enclosed several self-addressed envelopes for her use. She very kindly agreed to this scheme, and the letters began arriving quite regularly. The first few letters indicated that the Master was well, but by the third or fourth report she was referring to the Master's weakness and debility, although she also reported some talk of his undertaking a trip to Kanhangad. This was a bit confusing to me, since on the one hand he was being described as growing weaker, while on the other, plans for going to Kanhangad were being discussed. However, I was not distressed at the thought of a move to Kanhangad for several reasons. First, I recalled his telling me in 1944 that he would never be moving out of Ganeshpuri. Secondly, even if the move did take place, it would not affect me in the way it would the Bombay devotees, since I was accustomed to traveling some distance to see him in any event. Finally I planned to go to Bombay in early August and it was already mid-July. However I continued to experience unusual hallucinations all hinting at his final departure. It was an entirely unhappy period for me. The last letter from Mrs. Muktabai (dated August 4) reached me on the evening of August 7. It was a dark and rainy evening; I had planned to go to Sapru Hall to see a picture of Swami Yogananda, but after reading the letter I was very much depressed and remained at home. The letter said that the Master was very weak and that I should come immediately. Nevertheless it concluded as usual by saying that there was talk of his going to Kanhangad.

Only a few months prior to this, in December 1960, I had arranged a small altar in my home. A carpenter had fitted a shelf in a corner that was lit by the first rays of the morning sun. On this shelf I kept a framed photograph of the Master along with a silver lamp given to me by a friend. This lamp held just enough oil to burn for one hour without re-filling. It was my custom to light it every evening at sunset. Flowers were placed by the photograph as they were in season in our garden.

The next day, August 8, when I came home for lunch in the after-noon, I was quite surprised to find the little lamp burning in front of the Master's photograph; the picture was heavily garlanded as never be-fore with carefully woven ropes of flowers from the garden. In addi-tion, there were two vases each containing eight blue water lilies as well as a tray of *modaks*, a sweet traditionally prepared on the festival of the birth of Ganesh. When I asked my wife why she had arranged such a lavish display, she had no answer other than that she had felt like it. I had not shared my fears about the Master's passing with her, so her demonstration was all the more remarkable. She had begun to burn the oil lamp at 9:00 A.M. instead of the customary 7:00 P.M., and had kept it burning all day. She had collected all the available flowers, something she had never done before (nor indeed, after), including the sixteen lilies, and above all, prepared the modaks—and all without knowing why she was doing these things. The mystery was not solved until the next morning, when I received word of the Master's passing. Though I was absorbed in worldliness, the Master, full of love for his devotees, had sent this sign of his blessing at the time of casting away the physical form some nine hundred miles away.

In Ganeshpuri, during the fortnight the Master spent in the Bangalorewalla building he occupied a room on the eastern side of the building on the first floor, directly above the entrance. For the first three or four days, he did walk a little, though he was very weak. On July 27, 1961, his last Guru Purnima day, he addressed the assembled devotees. He spoke for nearly 45 minutes in his normal tone, even though he had been speaking in a weak whisper for several days. As mentioned earlier, he referred to the railroad engine and boxcars. He spoke of the uphill task that one faced (apparently of climbing the spiritual ascent, though each listener interpreted it in his own way) and the frequent slipping that could occur on the rails. He then advised that the cars must be kept firmly on the rails and the slipping overcome by throwing sand (probably detachment). Breaking loose from the engine could be prevented by forging bonds of unshakeable faith and conviction; the rest would happen "automatically." He made reference as well to the hospital being planned for Ganeshpuri which is further discussed in Appendix C.

A day or two later the Master was standing on the balcony with only Madhumama within hearing distance. The sun was about to set and the sky was comparatively clear for a July evening. He was heard saying, *"If anyone wants to see the sun, let him be seen now. Tomorrow he may not be seen."* The next day, the Master stopped moving around as he was growing weaker; he was now moved to the main hall where he remained until the mahasamadhi. It was a day without sunshine, cloudy and rainy.

At about 4:00 P.M. on the day before the mahasamadhi the Master asked for Mr. B.H. Mehta, popularly known as Babubhai Lokhandwalla. Mehta was having tea in a restaurant when the news came that the Master wanted him. He went immediately to the Master's room, where Nityananda gave him a large parcel tied in a piece of cloth and asked him to look after Kanhangad. Apparently the parcel contained cash, gold and other valuables. Subsequently it was Mr. Mehta who collected funds and constructed the two temples in Kanhangad, one above the rock-cut caves and the other at Guruvana.

The few words that were spoken by the Master on the last night of his earthly presence shed some light on the reasons that may have prompted him to take the first samadhi in the early twenties. On "coming back" he is reported to have said that he had left as *"the time was not yet."* In the last few months at Ganeshpuri, he was reported to be sad and in the last day or two almost tearful. Since many of those around him during the closing weeks and days were more concerned with worldly rather than spiritual matters, few were aware of the reasons. These reasons were perhaps not different from those described by Krishna in the *Gita:* "Whatever wish men bring me in worship, that wish I grant them....Most men worship gods because they want success in their worldly undertakings. This kind of material success can be gained very quickly here on earth. Fools pass blindly by the place of my dwelling. Who cares to seek for the perfect freedom?" The Nadigrantha reading extracted in Appendix A speaks of people coming to Nityananda for maya and not for higher values. The Master showed such seekers the truth of this by giving them relief and success in the mundane, both to relieve distress and as an incentive to seek that rarest gift he had the power to bestow. But this was not to be. Hence the sadness and the tearful departure. Readers may find it surprising or even shocking to realize that some people came to Ganeshpuri in order to find the correct number to gamble on by counting how many of the Master's fingers were visible at a given moment, or by counting the number of steps he took. It was mostly on such occasions that Nityananda would throw stones, shout, strike, or rebuke the person concerned. All the same, even those who got this sort of treatment received benefit.

Engineer Hegde had a sudden urge to go to Ganeshpuri on the evening of August 7. His family did not wish to accompany him, so he went alone. Gaining entry with some difficulty, he arrived in the samadhi hall just as Sandow Shetty was leaving with the doctor. Mr. Monappa was at the bedside. The doctor reported that everything was satisfactory and there was no need to worry about his health. This was just ten hours before the mahasamadhi.

As Shetty and the doctor were leaving, the doctor dropped his briefcase with a loud crash. The Master opened his eyes and asked what the noise was. After being informed, he asked who was standing at his feet and was told that it was Engineer Hegde. After a little while, he asked Monappa to go away. Hegde then started massaging his feet. This was around midnight; between midnight and 4:00 A.M. Hegde was alone with him. A little past midnight, the Master started speaking:

> *Everyone comes here for money and only money. The more they are given, the more they seek; there is no end to their greed. When they come they are pedestrians sometimes without a proper dwelling place; and when they get the necessities, then comforts and luxuries are demanded: a car, a bungalow, and so on. When earlier prayers are granted in the hope that contentment would follow and that they would then seek higher values, another demand is placed in a never-ending series of wants and desires. Not much point in allowing the body to continue—hence samadhi tomorrow.*

He repeated this last sentence three times. Hegde was stunned, for although the Master was very weak, the doctors had not found anything clinically wrong, and it was the general expectation that he would improve.

The Master then repeatedly asked where Swami Janananda was and why he had not come. This will always remain a mystery as he came only after the mahasamadhi and the dispatch of a cable. Hegde was deeply shocked; in tears he appealed to the Master to cancel or at least postpone the samadhi. Nityananda replied:

> *It is possible only if a few devotees come forward and make a request; not any devotees but those imbued with desireless devotion, feeling, and love* (nishkama bhakti, bhavana and prema). *Is there a* bhakta pundalika *around?* [Pundalika was a great devotee who made the Lord of Pandharpur wait for him.] *Even one such is enough and the samadhi will be canceled. When such a devotee is present, even God cannot*

> *take leave without his permission, or be able to disengage*
> *himself from the bond of his pure love.*

Then suddenly pointing his index finger at Engineer Hegde, he asked, *"Have you got nishkama bhakti?"* Hegde tearfully confessed that he did not have such unalloyed devotion. He told me that though he was a sincere devotee and would do anything ordered by the Master, he could not claim to be desireless.

During the remaining hour or so, the Master asked for two or three other persons who were available in Ganeshpuri. These could not be contacted readily or brought to the spot at that time of the night. Engineer Hegde was then asked not to worry about them. At about 3:45 A.M. or so the Master was again heard murmuring about Swami Janananda. Hegde asked the Master whether he could be of any service, but the Master replied in the negative, saying that only a sanyasi was suitable. At about 4:00 A.M. he told Hegde to go to the baths and then return. On his return, Hegde offered the Master some coffee. As he was about to pour it into the Master's mouth, the devotee in the next room woke up, and shouted at him to wait: he was planning to have a bath and then prepare coffee for the Master. The Master waved his hand as if to indicate that Hegde need not pour the coffee. As soon as the other devotee went for his bath, Hegde ran down to the hotel below and asked the Manager to get some special coffee quickly. The manager was very grateful for this rare opportunity. Shortly after serving this coffee to the Master, Hegde left, leaving the Master in the care of the other devotees who wished to serve him.

The time cannot be established exactly, but it was during the early morning that the Master ordered coffee and food for everyone assembled, perhaps so that they should not be inconvenienced by having to delay their next meal once he attained mahasamadhi. Mr. Lakshmansa Khoday, who came from Bangalore, arrived sometime during this period.

Three months earlier the Ashram kitchen had been closed. Since then, the Master would order sugar cane juice for all visiting devotees. When Mrs. Muktabai commented on this one day, he replied, *"Sugar cane juice? It is this one's juice."* Perhaps he meant that it was the outward expression of his love and sweetness towards all devotees and the devout, as a prelude to the final departure. In the last months, coffee and food were ordered for all visiting devotees instead of sugar cane juice.

Among the visiting devotees who assembled at about 6:00 that morning was Chandu, a companion devotee for many years from Kanhangad. He had arrived a few days earlier. The Master asked him whether he had brought *kasthuri* (a kind of musk oil). Chandu burst into tears upon hearing this, for years ago in Kanhangad the Master had told him that when he asked for kasthuri it would be time for his departure. To pacify him, the Master asked whether Chandu would take him to Kanhangad and whether there were any trains. Chandu in his simplicity confirmed that there were trains. The Master then asked how he could go in his present condition with no strength in his legs (this is a common way of expressing that the body was weak). He repeated this question.

After 7:00 A.M., some of the women devotees from the early days wished to wait on the Master. Mrs. Wagle, a professional nurse, took the lead in this last service to the Master.

Mr. C.C. Parekh had accepted an offer of a lift to Bombay. He planned to leave Ganeshpuri around 7:00 on the morning of the 8th, ride to Bombay just to inform his people that he would be staying at Ganeshpuri for a few days, and return to the Ashram that same afternoon. Before getting into the car, he thought he should have the Master's darshan; asking his friend to wait for a moment, he went up to the hall where the Master was resting. He was shocked to find the Master breathing with great difficulty, struggling for breath. He administered oxygen and the breathing improved, but seeing the Master's condition, Parekh gave up the idea of going to Bombay. He remained standing at the head of the bed and was soon joined by Dr. Nicholson, a well-known eye specialist of Bombay and a devotee of the Master. Soon the doctor's wife joined them. She had gone to call the doctor from the neighboring sanatorium. The doctor came, examined the Master, and prescribed some medicines. These were not administered. Sometime later Nityananda asked for the oxygen mask to be removed; his breathing was normal. He asked Parekh for a little water and took a few sips.

At about 8:45 A.M. he asked Mr. Lakshmansa Khoday for a little fresh lemon juice. Khoday gave him some tender coconut water, which was accepted. This is thought to be the last intake the Master had, and was perhaps an indication of the service the house of Khoday would be destined to render to the principal Ashrams run in Nityananda's name.

At about 9:30 A.M. Gopalmama noticed that the Master's body was very hot. When he conveyed this to him, the Master replied, *"It will be like that,"* implying that it was the normal condition at that stage. He then repeated words that he had reportedly said often in the last months: *"Sadhu became Swami; Swami became Deva* [God] *to some, Baba and Bhagawan* [God] *to others; Deva will now enter samadhi, sthira* [constant] *samadhi."* According to Gopalmama these were the last audible words uttered by the Master about an hour before entering mahasamadhi.

According to Parekh, between 10:40 and 10:45 A.M. the Master took two or three very deep breaths. The last breath was so deep that his chest became fully expanded. He straightened his legs as far as possible (he could not straighten one of them fully due to arthritis), joined his hands a little above his navel, and moved no more. After a short time, Parekh called Swami Muktananda and others from the adjoining room to take charge of the body for whatever rituals had to be performed. The Master had left his earthly body.

Between the afternoon of the 8th and the evening of the 9th, there was a great deal of discussion about where the holy remains should be interred. The devotee who had constructed Kailas with funds provided by the Master had planned a subterranean room for the samadhi and thought interment should be there. The reasons that prompted him in his proposal were not acceptable to the others. Some others suggested that a special samadhi be constructed on the hill behind the present museum building. Yet another group of devotees felt that since the Master had especially come to the Bangalorewalla building for the mahasamadhi, the interment should take place on the spot. Mr. Khoday said that it would be his proud privilege to have a suitable structure constructed, should the majority decide to have the interment in the Bangalorewalla building.

There was still another group who argued that the body should be interred in the original Ashram of the Master, and ultimately this view prevailed. Earlier it was mentioned that the Master had ordered the slab put on the new walls in this Ashram in considerable haste. Had this slab not been affixed, the holy remains could not have been interred there during the rains of this monsoon season. It would therefore appear that the Master knew his physical remains would be laid to rest there. He often said that all the sages were around the old Ashram.

◇   ◇   ◇

On the morning of August 9, a phone message awaited me at my office. I called home and learned that a telegram had arrived from Mrs. Muktabai saying that the Master had attained mahasamadhi on the 8th and that interment would be in three days. Had I not been in correspondence with Mrs. Muktabai, no one would have advised me of the event. I later learned that the Master had attained mahasamadhi at about 10:45 the previous day. So the worst had happened.

Through circumstances which could be considered semi-miraculous, I found myself in Bombay by 11:00 P.M. that same night. There I learned that the holy remains would be interred at 8:00 the next morning, August 10. I didn't know if I could get there by that early hour; the last local train for Virar had already left, and no taxi would oblige, as the road was neither sound nor safe past Thana at that time of night. To make matters worse there was a steady drizzle. After trying until midnight to arrange some transportation, I finally spent the night with a friend and caught the first local train to Virar on the morning of the 10th. I reached Bassein (Vasai Road now) at about 5:30 A.M. only to find a line of some 150 people all wanting to go to Ganeshpuri. The State Transport Office was closed, and the whole area looked desolate and deserted except for the crowd of devotees. I joined the line and was slowly preparing myself to face the fact that I might not be able to have a last glimpse of the Master's physical form, even though I was now only 25 miles away.

As I was thus musing, a group of five people moved out of the line and hailed a taxi which was coming from Bassein, but the driver was not willing to take the trip, and they rejoined the line. However, the sheer hopelessness of standing in an impossible line drove me out of it, and I started pacing up and down from the station to the fork in the road: to the right lay Ganeshpuri and to the left Bassein and the Fort. After pacing this 200 yard stretch several times, I again approached the fork in the road. This time I saw an old seven-seater coming from Bassein. I hailed the driver and asked whether he would take me to Ganeshpuri. He quoted a reasonable rate for that time of the day, and I invited six others from the crowd to join me. On the way, the driver repeated at least three times: "You are a lucky person. This is not my usual run and yet I am taking you." It sounded as though he were making the trip in spite of himself. He dropped us in front of the Bhadrakali temple at about 7:15 A.M. The driver then just wheeled around and disappeared as fast as he had come, even though normally a hired vehicle would try to get passengers for the return trip.

I was overjoyed to have arrived. There was such a crowd that I did not know where to look for the body of the Master. At that time I was not aware that he had moved to the Bangalorewalla building, in fact, I was not even aware that the building had been constructed. Somehow I managed to push through the crowd and five minutes later saw at a distance that the Master's body was being carried out of the Bangalorewalla building and placed on a jeep. The rays of the sun broke through the clouds lighting up his face; I could not say that he had left the body. Though he had grown very thin and weak at the time of the mahasamadhi, on this morning, his body did not appear emaciated.

I immediately rushed forward and caught hold of the jeep as I learned that there would be a procession around the buildings before proceeding to the old Ashram for interment. In the meantime, the clouds closed in again and there was a slight drizzle throughout the last journey. It took more than an hour to reach the eastern entrance of the old Ashram. The body was seated in the lotus position and had been placed on an easy chair, which was carried by means of two logs tied to the arms. As I never released my hold on the jeep throughout this period, I got my last glimpse of the Master at close quarters as the easy chair was lowered and taken inside the low roof.

There was no possibility of entering the old Ashram as it was filled and overflowing. Instead, I went for a bath and then to pray. I was deeply gratified that the samadhi was situated at the very place I used to rest during my occasional visits from outstations, after the Master moved into Kailas. For the first time I truly understood and appreciated his words to me that *"that alone is good."* I was deeply grateful for his grace.

Conclusion

Nityananda of Ganeshpuri was a perfect living example of renunciation and of the Vedantic wisdom of universal oneness. He lived with no distinctions, no separations. He was often right in the midst of the poor and the backward, from his earliest days in South Kanara to his last days in Ganeshpuri, yet the higher classes also followed him. Indeed, it is to the courtesy of some of these devotees of the South Kanara era that I owe much of the early narrative. In Ganeshpuri also, he was surrounded by the high and the low. He was the common man's friend, the spiritual aspirant's guide, and the devotee's eternal companion. He taught that devotion to God must be blended with the efficient performance of one's duties, and insisted on devotion to work. He would say that work properly performed is as good as worship. In the *Chidakash Gita,* he quoted the homely example of a cashew nut—attached to the fruit and yet not buried in its flesh like the seeds of other fruits. Similarly the Master wanted a good devotee to be in the world without being worldly. Secondly, he set an example for all who knew him of how charitable work should be done—with a sense of offering and as an opportunity to serve God. It is for this reason that he was so fond of feeding the poor; he also built a small school in Ganeshpuri and a dispensary in Vajreshwari. While karmic law is responsible for the suffering of individuals and nations, it does not justify callousness or indifference towards the needy and the suffering.

For the rest, the seeker only need have shuddha bhavana and shraddha, allowing the Master a free hand to work from within. He needed no gifts, money, or estate; what was offered was freely distributed and the rest was never secured. The greatness of a guru such as Nityananda lies in the key he holds to the inner consciousness of the faithful, without having to deliver speeches or write books; radiating power all the time, without an overt effort or indication that such radiation was taking place. To use the description in the *Bhagawatam*, the Divine Power of such a guru remains hidden at times, but becomes manifest before those who adore the Truth .

His pure transparency rendered him open to manifestation in different forms to different people, reflecting their own inner state of consciousness—showing as a mirror does the exact reflection of the object held before it. Always he was in the same mood: if one found him in moods, these were reflections of the viewer's own state. There can be no partitioning of reality; duality is only an intellectual distinction. The sun is not separate from its light, water from its wetness or fire from its heat. If some saw the terror of Kali in him, others equally found in him the peace and compassion of Vajreshwari.

In the last few months of his earthly sojourn, Nityananda often remarked to the old devotees that everyone came for the grace of the guru, but all they wanted was the fulfillment of some material desire. And even when one desire was granted, fulfillment of another was sought. He would then ask, *"What sort of grace could be bestowed in such cases?"* He said they did not need a guru but a soothsayer. To quote him as reported, they would even shit on their palms and seek instructions for its disposal. On such occasions the Master told the other devotees that this was an abuse of his physical presence. In the Nadi-grantha extract in Appendix A, it is said that many went to him for maya and not for higher values. He himself said they came window-shopping. They came to the ocean only to catch a few readily available fish, not to dive deep for the pearls lying below.

Nityananda's own words describe the right attitude and the right behavior: [14]

> One must live in the world like common men. An-
> tarjnanis don't go in for miracles. It does not mean that a
> realized person can jump into a well or from a high
> mountain without anything happening to him, or that if a
> rag is tied to his hand and soaked in kerosene and lighted,
> that it would not burn. [Perhaps the Master had in mind
> the incident of Padabidri.] Jnanis also suffer from pain like
> all others, but they have the capacity to keep their minds
> completely detached from the nerve centers. Hence they
> might remember the pain once or twice in a day. Once
> one is established in Infinite Consciousness, one be-
> comes silent, and though knowing everything, goes
> about as if he does not know anything. Though he might
> be doing a lot of things in several places, to all outward
> appearance, he will remain as if he does nothing. He will
> always remain as if he is a witness to everything that goes
> on, like a spectator at a cinema show, and is not affected
> by the pleasant or the unpleasant. To be able to forget ev-
> erything and be aloof, that alone is the highest state to be
> in.

When asked how one should keep one's mind, he said:

> It should be like a lotus leaf, which though in water, with
> its stem in the mud and the flower above, is yet untouched
> by both. Similarly the mind should be kept untainted by
> the mud of desires and the water of distractions, even
> though engaged in worldly activities. Then, just as the
> stalk, stem, and leaf, when properly cultivated and not
> disturbed, will culminate in the lotus blossom, similarly if
> the detached mind and faith in the Sadguru (God or his in-
> carnation) are firmly established in the lotus of the heart,
> and never allowed to wax or wane with happiness and
> difficulties, his grace will be invoked. There are various

---

[14]Portions of this talk have been reproduced earlier in the narrative.

tests to which a devotee is subjected: they could be of the mind, of the intellect, of the body and so on. A number of such tests are there. In fact God is conducting tests all the time; every occurrence in life is a test. Every thought that crops up in the mind is in itself a test to see what one's reaction will be. Hence one must be always alert and aloof, conducting oneself with a spirit of detachment, viewing everything as an opportunity afforded to gain experience, to improve onself and go on to a higher stage. Desires are the only cause of sorrows in this world. Nothing is brought into this world and nothing can be taken. There are for instance so many things in this Ashram. They are all meant for use by devotees visiting the place. If this one goes elsewhere, none of these things would be taken. Whatever is needed there will come separately. This one is not flattered because some important persons have visited, or depressed because someone that used to come has not turned up. Whether people who come here offer or do not offer anything, it is the same. There is no desire to go anywhere or see anything, nor is there any longing for any visitors to come. Whatever one says must be reflected in one's thinking and actions. If one is advised to be like a lotus leaf, that is because of the practice prevailing here. There is not even the desire to do good to anyone. Everything that happens, happens automatically by the will of God. Nevertheless if any one is genuinely interested, some words come out of this one.

It is with love and humility that these words of and about the Master are offered to you, the reader:

May the blessings of Nityananda be on all devotees and the devout— past, present, or future, in India and outside, without distinction of faith or caste, creed or country.

Appendixes

Fate, Stars and Numbers

Stars: The Nadigrantha Reading

In March, 1970 a Bombay astrologer was consulted for a Nadigrantha reading of this devotee's horoscope. Such readings are drawn up by sages with intuitive wisdom who chart all possible permutations and combinations to develop the pattern of the subject's life; that is the Nadigrantha reading.

These astrological readings cover all possible nativities in great detail. They even contain the names of the individuals, and the names and charts of those that have influenced the individual for good or evil. They include references to incidents in previous incarnations that have brought about the present situation—happy or otherwise. However, experience indicates that these readings are correct only as they relate to the past. Their predictive part often proves to be incorrect, perhaps because the chart is an assessment and a challenge, rather than a final pronouncement, allowing for the play of human will power and divine intervention.

In this particular reading, the astrologer recorded that when the native was 28 years old, he would meet a great being. There followed a lengthy description of this person, which is reproduced below in two versions. The first column contains many of the original Sanskrit terms and phrases; the second column contains a paraphrased and edited version. I crave the indulgence of scholars, if the Sanskrit words have been erroneously recorded.

original

Darshan of such a guru is *durlabh*. *Kevala Paramatma Avatar.* He came down only for the sake of devotees. *Parama Sakshatkar. Yogi, yogi, mahaan yogi, Samartha Ishwar Avatar.* Nothing known of his birth. No one knows his age: Guru Maha *Samarth: Maha Avadhooth Purush. Datta, Shiva and Parabrahma,* all in one.

Fond of *Anna Daan: Anna Poorna (Goddess Parvati)* behind him. Has fed thousands of Sanyasis and *Digambar* Sadhus at Triveni during *Kumba Melas,* and other Holy Teerthas.

Always in Samadhi—but talks. Always with the Atman, not in the body. Directly talks to Paramatma. Always in contact with the Supreme.

Long-limbed with a resplendent personality. Sometimes would wear nothing and at other times a langoti. Parabrahma in human form but few know him. No one knows his age.

His known name begins with the letter *N.* He sits near hot springs and a Shiva Mandir. Shiva Avatar. *Swayam Praapti.* Does not engage himself with outward activities, and hence gave the impression of not doing anything. Took money from his langoti. Remover of difficulties. Would prescribe medicines on occasion. *Ajnanis* (ignorant persons) who went there did not know his true nature or greatness.

Poorna, Sampoorna, Paripoorna, Samartha, Avatara Purusha. Maya and Brahma in his hand.

This description is too brief in relation to his status and greatness. For a proper description, a devotee will come in due course. If any one writes about him, it can succeed only if it is his wish and is done with his inspiration. Like *Valmiki Ramayana,* a

edited

He came down only for the sake of devotees. Great yogi. Nothing is known of his birth. No one knows his age. He has fed thousands of sanyasis and sadhus.

He is always in samadhi—but talks. He is always with the Atman—not in the body. He talks directly to the Supreme.

He is long-limbed with a resplendent personality. He sometimes wears nothing, and at other times a loincloth. He is the Supreme in human form but few know him. No one knows his age.

His known name begins with the letter *N.* He sits near hot springs and a Shiva Mandir: he does not engage in outward activities, and hence gives the impression of not doing anything. He takes money from his loincloth. He removes difficulties. He prescribes medicines on occasion. Ignorant persons do not know his true nature or greatness.

This description is too brief in relation to his status and greatness. For a proper description, a devotee will come in due course. Anyone who writes about him will succeed only if it is his wish, and is done with his inspiration. Literature will be written about him in due course.

He is no longer in his human form. Already many ashrams and temples have been built in his name and for him. He has many followers but no disciples adopted and initiated as such. No one was fit to receive the Brahma Vidya from him. After him, many will make money in his name. He has no disciples, only devotees. His unknown devotees include highly evolved sanyasis and even members of the royalty.

Sahitya (literature) will be written about him in due course.

He is no longer in his human frame. Already many ashrams and temples have been built in his name and for him. He has many followers but no *shishya*s (disciples) adopted and initiated as such. No one was fit to receive the *Brahma Vidya* from him. After him, many will make money in his name. As in the case of Rama and Krishna, hypocrites will flourish in his name. But he has no disciples, only devotees. His unknown devotees include highly evolved sanyasis and even members of the royalty.

Though in mahasamadhi now, his blessings are with the devotees. Even if you think of him intensely, he is there. Everyone that comes to him with purity of motive gets his wish fulfilled. Samartha purusha—how can he be described?

Will be scolding and beating sometimes. But benediction to those at the receiving end. Says *"Matti, matti."* (Literally, dust; meaning as of no consequence or useless.)

Viewed everyone with *sama-dhrishti* (equalsightedness) and accorded equal treatment to everyone, big or small. Persons went to him for maya, not for higher values. *Akshaya Paramatma*—in *Kali Yuga* his guiding light will always be available to guide the devout and the spiritual aspirants. But most of his devotees never knew him.

No one powerful enough to succeed him or to receive what he could have vouchsafed. Even now blessing the devotees. Has no shishyas, only bhaktas.

Though in mahasamadhi now, his blessings are with the devotees. When you think of him intensely, he is there. Everyone who comes to him with purity of motive, gets his wish fulfilled. How can he be described?

Sometimes there are scoldings and beatings, but benediction comes to those at the receiving end. He says *"Matti, matt,"* (literally, dust; of no consequence or useless).

He views everyone with equal-sightedness, and accords equal treatment to everyone, big or small. People approached him for maya, not for higher values. His guiding light will always be available to help guide the devout, and the spiritual aspirants. But most of his devotees never knew him.

No one is powerful enough to succeed him, or to receive what he could have vouchsafed. Even now he blesses the devotees. He has no disciples, only devotees.

It was a thrilling experience on that warm March afternoon in 1970 to listen to this astoundingly accurate description being read by the astrologer. When I went for the reading, I had an uncanny feeling that I would be listening to a description of the Master of Ganeshpuri and this proved correct. Perhaps it was also divine will that I should hear about him in this way, and others through me. Many of the qualities attributed to the Master in this reading are well known to his devotees, and many are reflected in the incidents related in this book.

Fate and Numbers

When the young Master became known in South Kanara, his devotees were genuinely eager to ascertain details like the date and year of his birth, so that a horoscope could be cast. His gruff reply was always the same: *"Is this one going to be at the mercy of astrologers? What is the necessity and relevance of ascertaining how, when, and where the body came from; it is enough if the body is seen and the result experienced: one who sees this one once will not forget."*

However, although nothing is known of the details of the Master's birth, there is a noteworthy numerological feature in the dates of his mahasamadhi and of subsequent events connected with the consecration of his statue and inauguration of the Samadhi Mandir, though none of the events were planned in this way. All of these occurred under the number 8. Nityananda took mahasamadi on 8-8-61 ($1+9+6+1=17$, i.e., $1+7=8$), i.e., three 8s. As the mahasamadhi took place between 10:40 and 10:45 AM (I have checked with Mr. Parekh, who was present at the bedside), the time could have been 10:43 ($1+0+4+3=8$). The Samadhi Mandir was inaugurated exactly 11 years and 6 months after the mahasamadhi ($11+6=17$, i.e., $1+7=8$), on 8-2-73. The *muhurth*, or the exact time fixed by the Pandits for the consecration of the statue was 12:50 PM on this date ($1+2+5+0=8$).

According to Cheiro and other scholars of numerology, the number eight has a special significance. Its two circles represent the material and the spiritual, the pleasant and the good. The lower circle of the number eight could therefore represent the outer court yard. It was perhaps to this difference that the Master referred when in his last earthly days he would sadly remark that everyone came for the grace of the guru, yet all they could aspire to ask was the fulfillment of some material desire. Only when one passes through and transcends this lower circle of worldliness can one enter the upper circle. The samadhi shrine of Nityananda represents the upper circle at Ganeshpuri. The hungry adivasi children, persons in distress, and persons seeking spirituality, can only find solace and satisfaction here.

As a postscript, when I completed this manuscript and took t to Ganeshpuri on Guru Purnima day for dedication at the Master's mahasamadhi, I observed that it fell this year on the 17th of July. An idle curiosity prompted me to count the number of letters in the original title of this book and I was astonished to find that they added up to 26 (2 + 6 = 8). However the numerical value of the letters comes to 24, or 6, the number of Venus, the representative of Love, just as the three eights mentioned earlier add up to 24 or 6.

I have not recorded these observations to provide any comparisons but only to furnish data to help a future student of the occult to make his own inferences. The Master himself would have perhaps admonished me for such digressive dilettantism!

In Praise of Nityananda

Many devotees have been inspired by the sight of the Master and by association with him to spontaneously create songs or poetry in praise of him. The devotees so inspired were not necessarily even literate, and those who were educated did not always produce writings in their native language.

Mrs. Krishnabai started producing such inspirational lines in praise of the Master in the mid-twenties in Mangalore. There was no particular time for the effusion, and the language in which she expressed herself was Marathi. She did not know Marathi and hence wrote it in Kanarese script. The inspiration did not come regularly or predictably, and could be either prose or poetry. The inspiration ceased by the mid-seventies. Some of her inspired writings have been printed for free distribution to devotees.

Mr. Mhasker, priest for the Samadhi Shrine at Ganeshpuri, has composed many inspirational songs of praise *(bhajan)* for the Master in the Marathi tongue. The bhajan sung for the main arathi at Ganeshpuri was composed by him; it is used at some of the other temples dedicated to the Master as well.

Professor R. Bendre of Dharwar is a famed expert in both literature and mathematics who has won several Sahitya Academy awards. The professor, a devotee of Sri Aurobindo, visited Ganeshpuri in 1966 in response to an invitation by the Trustees. When I met him in October 1969, he spoke of having been inspired to write quite a few poems on Nityananda; he said the dominant image was of light.

Mr. Mudbhatkal tells of his first visit to Ganeshpuri along with a few friends. It was quite late by the time they took leave of the Master; Mudbhatkal rode in the back seat of the crowded car. It was nearly midnight when they passed through Bhiwandi. Suddenly they were bombarded with a fusillade of stones; several crashed through the windscreen, slightly injuring the man at the wheel. Despite his injury, the driver did not stop, but drove off at high speed. They saw a large unruly gang lying in wait at the side of road. Mudbhatkal was certain that if the driver had hesitated at all, they would have been stopped, looted, and beaten. The driver later confessed that he did not know what reflexes had operated causing him to continue driving though injured.

By the time Mudbhatkal arrived at his home, it was 2:00 A.M.; but as he was having his bath, he suddenly felt an inspiration and called for pencil and paper. He wrote out a two line stanza in Sanskrit which praised Nityananda. By his own report, though he had read Sanskrit as a second language many years before, his field was chemistry and his knowledge of Sanskrit was "not worth knowing." From this time on for the next three months, such inspirations would arise, coming at any time or place. Mudbhatkal soon learned to keep pencil and paper handy at all times. After three months and a hundred stanzas, the inspiration stopped. He told me that he has shown the verses to Sanskrit scholars who were surprised that the rhyme and meter were nearly perfect. The scholars advised against changing the verses to be technically perfect, saying that they should remain as written, with their refreshing originality. The stanzas are proposed to be published under the name *Nityananda Shatakam*.

Mrs. Krishnabai recalled that scores of devotees of both sexes would gather round the youthful Nityananda in Mangalore, and some would burst into song in praise of him. Many of them were not intelligible to her as they appeared to be compositions in Tamil, Telegu, Malayalam, and so on. Occasionally, someone would go into a trance and address Nityananda in the highest terms, generally asserting that he was a God on earth. She recalled one such statement: "You are *Dattatreya*; you do not know who you are. You gave mukti to two people the other day. Please give me mukti." The Master never responded directly when so addressed. He would turn away, and then after some time he would ask the host to serve the devotees tender coconut water. All would be quiet after drinking it.

APPENDIX C

Sri Nityananda Arogyashram Hospital at Ganeshpuri

The beginnings of Sri Nityananda Arogyashram are in a way connected with the late Dr. M.B. Cooper and the herbal wonder drug, the formula of which was revealed to him by a saint from the Himalayas over six decades ago, soon after he had returned from England where he had completed his medical studies. By his own genius and through the vibrationary guidance he received from time to time, he successfully prepared an injectable solution from the original formula. Though originally given as a specific for tuberculosis, Dr. Cooper remembered the saint saying that in the Himalayan regions they drank this herba extract as a specific for all diseases and what is more, for general health and strength. With this as his guide, he continued to study this compound and finally discovered its wide-spectrum curative properties. As a result, in his long and successful career he was able to cure thousands of patients suffering from several diseases: all types of lung ailments including asthma, skin diseases, arthritis and cysts; all in addition to tuberculosis of all varieties, even in advanced stages. Hence he named the medicine *mahawaz* (the great sound), after the sound that constantly seemed to direct him in his researches.

Dr. Deodhar worked as Dr. Cooper's assistant from the late thirties and practiced the administration of this medicine. In the late forties, Dr. Deodhar met Sadguru Nityananda and subsequently became his great devotee. He eventually left his general practice and concentrated on mahawaz as a result of the advice sought and received from the

163

great Master. He was also told in reply to his query that the medicine could become a great healer if administered through the hospital but that much patience and perseverence would be needed.

After a time, Dr. Deodhar and Mr. B.C.S. Swamy , who were both devotees of Sadguru Nityananda, decided to take Dr. Cooper to Ganeshpuri to seek the Master's benediction for the development of the medicine and later for establishing a hospital in the area. The story of this first meeting of Dr. Cooper and the Master has already been re-counted; the doctor was overwhelmed by the greatness of Nityananda. When he returned to Ganeshpuri, he brought an ampule of mahawaz to show the Master. Nityananda said that it would succeed but it would take time. With this benediction, the idea of establishing an Arogy-ashram with a hospital at Ganeshpuri began to take shape.

Soon thereafter, a few months before the mahasamadhi, Dr. Deodhar and Mr. Swamy brought a proposal for a hospital at Ganeshpuri before the Master. The idea not only received his approval but he immediately called for a plan of the Ashram Estate. On that he indicated the area where the future hospital should be constructed; an outright grant of the land was made on the spot as well as an additional cash donation. He also indicated that the hospital should be built in three stages, illustrating with his hands: "first small, then bigger and then very big."

The Nityananda Arogyashram Trust was constituted in 1963 and in December 1966 the foundation stone of the hospital was laid by Swami Chinmayananda in the presence of a distinguished gathering. It is one of the finest hospital buildings in the district, with spacious airy rooms and is situated in idyllic surroundings just a walking distance from the Nityananda Samadhi Mandir.

Before his death, Dr. Cooper donated the formula of the mahawaz to the Sri Nityananda Arogyashram trust. Both Dr. Cooper and later Dr. Deodhar had fabulous offers for this formula, but as the avowed objec-tive was to manufacture and market it in a way that made it available to the common man, they refused to allow it to be commercialized. With the same spirit both his daughter Dr. M.H. Pavri, and son Mr. Cooper gave up rights to any royalties they might be entitled on this account. With the passing away of Dr. Deodhar in August 1980, sole responsi-bility for running the hospital and for the manufacture and develop-ment of mahawaz has devolved to Dr. Pavri. She spends four days a week at Ganeshpuri and together with the Resident Medical Officer at-tends to the outpatients and treats a large number with mahawaz. She also treats a large number of mahawaz patients in Bombay. Dr. Pavri is working in an honorary capacity and donates to the hospital any monies received from mahawaz patients.

Future plans include the immediate opening of a department for the treatment of arthritis and related conditions (e.g., rheumatic, rheumatoid and osteo-arthritis, spondilitis) and skin diseases (e.g., pernicious eczema, psoriasis). Patients who are crippled or incapacitated with arthritis will be treated with hot sulphur spring water baths, modern physiotherapy, and mahawaz.

All of this requires funds; to this end, the net proceeds from the sale of this book will be credited to the Sri Nityananda Hospital Trust.

About the Author

Mr. M.U. Hatengdi was born at Mangalore in December 1914, had his early education in the local G.H. School and Government College, and obtained his Honours/Masters degree in Economics from the Presidency College, Madras in 1936.

Joining the Indian Navy in 1941, he retired in 1964. At the time of retirement, Capt. Hatengdi was the Naval Secretary at Naval Headquarters, New Delhi. He was immediately appointed as the Commercial Manager in the Government-owned Mazagaon Dock and soon after was selected as the General Manager and Chairman of the Board of Administration of one of the largest buying and selling agencies of the government, known as the Canteen Stores Department, from which he retired in July 1970.

He has since been interesting himself in activity connected with social organizations and religious trusts.

Glossary

The definitions in this glossary are limited to the specific context of this book and do not claim to be authoritative. In the case of transliteration inconsistencies between the South Indian usage followed in this text and classic Sanskrit, the Sanskrit spelling is given in italics.

acharya   teacher

adivasi   tribal people

ajnani   one without wisdom; ignorant one

ananda   literally, bliss; this is the traditional ending for names of initiates of certain orders of monks

anna daan   anna : food; daan : charity or distribution

Annapoorna   aspect of Mother Parvati as the Complete Feeder

antarjnani   antar : inner; jnani : one who knows; one who has attained divine wisdom

arathi   (Sanskrit *arati*) light; the ritual of waving a light and incense before a holy picture, statue, or place

Arjuna   hero of the *Mahabharata*; the teaching of the *Bhagavad Gita* was given to him by Krishna

arrack   fermented beverage from the sap of the toddy palm; a country drink

ashirvad   blessing

ashram   a stage of life; retreat; a place for spiritual exercise, instruction, and practice

ashtagraha yoga   astha : eight, graha : grasping, holding; as astrological term, refers to time when all planets are aligned in one sign

ashtasiddhi   ashta : 8, siddhi : literally, accomplishment; here occult power acquired through discipline

atman   Self, Absolute; also the individual self; essence

avadhuta   one who is God-mad; does not keep a fixed residence, may appear eccentric, is not aware of dirt or cleanliness, of hunger or sleep; and is neither attracted nor repelled by the dualities of the phenomenal world

avatar   consciously willed descent of spirit into matter; the Supreme Spirit assuming human form

Ayurveda   ancient Hindu art of medicine and prolonged life; ayu : life, veda : knowledge

—bai   suffix rendering a name into the feminine gender; same as —amma and — deva

Bal Bhojan   literally, feeding of young boys; here refers to providing meals to poor children

Benares   also *Banares* and *Banaras*; now officially called *Varanasi*; also called *Kashi*, meaning City of Light; it is a very holy place for Hindus; to die in Benares, to be burned on its sacred ghats and to have one's ashes scattered into the holy river is thought to put an immediate end to the cycles of death and rebirth, thus, liberation.

Bhadrakali   a goddess

Bhagawan   godhead; one who possess the six treasures; one who is full of light

Bhagawatam   life of Krishna written by Vyasa

Bhagavad Gita   *Divine Song*; part of the *Mahabharata*, written between 200 BC and AD 200 (dates disputed)

bhajans   devotional songs

bhakti   devotion; selfless devotion to god as a means of attaining liberation

bhavana   feeling; emotion, sensitivity; creative contemplation

Bhimeshwar   a god; Bhima, "the mighty one," was a brother of Arjuna

Brahman   one of the many Indian terms used to describe pure undifferentiated consciousness; the Ultimate

Brahma vidya   knowledge of God

brahmin   the first and highest of the four orders of traditional Indian society; priests belong to this order

Brahmarandra   literally, the opening to God in the head; the place where the spinal column meets the brain

chaddar   versatile strip or square of cloth used as a shawl or blanket, etc.

chaturmas   chatur : four; literally, four months; the four months of monsoon during which, traditionally, wandering sadhus would stay in one place; now a period spent in special study.

Chidakash Gita   title of a collection of the sayings of Nityananda; chid : consciousness compared to the sky, akasha : space, Gita : song; implies a space or state in which perception is objectless

dandha   literally, stick, as in "stick of justice;" in this usage refers to duty or experiences that must be lived out

darshan   literally, seeing; in particular the act of seeing the divinity within the guru or within the representation of the divine as in a sculpture or painting; a system of philosophy

datta devata siddhi   Datta : great sage who embodied the trinity of Brahma, Vishnu, and Shiva; deva : god/goddess; siddhi : power acquired through spiritual practice

Devi   literally, a shining one; goddess (deva : god)

digamber   nude

drishti   sight

durlabh   very rare, almost impossible

Ganesha   elephant headed son of Shiva and Parvati
ghee   a form of clarified butter used in Hindu rituals; also widely used in Indian cooking
Gopala   form of Krishna as the cow-tender
gopi   a milkmaid; Krishna danced and played with Gopis
Govinda   literally, giver of enlightenment; name of Krishna
gramadevata   village deity (grama : village)
Gujarat   province on NW coast of India, north of Bombay
guru   the teacher, esp. spiritual teacher perceptor giving personal religious instructions
Guru Purnima   festival of the guru; held in July on the full moon night
Guruvana   jungle area near Kanhangad; legend has it that the infant Nityananda was found abandoned here; today it is the site of a temple dedicated to Nityananda

Haj   pilgrimage to Mecca; a Moslem holy event
halwa   sweet confection common in the middle and far east
harijan   untouchable
harikatha   sacred story told in song and narrative; hari : god; katha : story

Indra   chief god in the Vedic pantheon
Ishwara   simply, Lord or deity

japa   mantra repetition
jnani   one who knows; wise one; one who has attained divine wisdom *(jnana)*; wisdom acquired through meditation

Kailas   mountain in the Himalayas called the home of Shiva; the name of Nityananda's second ashram in Ganeshpuri which he occupied from 1956 to 1961
Kali Yuga   the present age; fourth in a series as given in ancient Hindu texts
kamandalu   water container traditionally carried by wandering sadhus
karma   action itself; action done with desire for results, the fruits of which are either being manifested or accumulated
kasthuri   (Sanskrit *kasturi*) musk
koti-teertha   teertha : holy place; koti : crore : 10 million; thus, very holy places
kumkum   vermilion powder used in rituals
kundalini   the creative power of Shiva as it is manifest in the individual; literally, coiled up
kunds (*kunda*)   hot springs; baths

langoti   loincloth
linga   literally, sign; short column, resembling a phallus, often with a cobra head behind it; in Hindu worship, it is a symbol of Shiva and the masculine principle

maha   great

Mahabharata   ancient Hindu epic collection; contains 18 books, including the *Bhagavad Gita*

mahapurusha   purusha : person, male, one's true self; regarded as eternal and unaffected by external happenings; maha : great; indicates one who resides always in this true and unchanging self

mahasamadhi   literally, great resolution, resolving; when speaking of a saint, it is the conscious shedding of the physical body

mahawaz   name given by Dr. Cooper to the medicine used at the Nityananda Arogyashram hospital

mandir   temple

mantra   sacred word or formula to be chanted; that sacred word or formula by which the nature of the Supreme is reflected on as identical with the self.

mantrasiddhi   powers that arise from mantra repetition

mantravadi   one who repeats mantra; one who believes in doctrine of mantra; derivatively, one who has attained extraordinary power through use of mantra repetition

math   monastery

mathadipathi   leader of a math; abbot

Matsyendranath   great sage of the Nath order

matti   literally, dust; of no consequence, useless

maya   literally, that which measures; power which produces sense of difference and diverse objects; the appearance and experience of duality

modaks   traditional food prepared at the feast for the birth of Ganesh

moksha   absolute freedom from bondage

mukti   liberation from bondage

Naag   snake, particularly a cobra; seen in Shiva shrines

Nandi   a bull; Shiva's vehicle

nityananda eternal bliss; nitya : constant, continuous

padmasana   the lotus posture of hatha yoga; often described as an ideal seated position of meditation

para   supreme (usually seen as a prefix)

parabrahma   supreme deity; God

paramatma   supreme soul; God

Parvati   goddess; consort of Shiva

pipal   a fig tree native to India; with its multiple descending roots it resembles the banyan tree of the west

pooja   worship or ritual; a more modern spelling is *puja*

poorna   full

prasad   consecrated food given by a deity or guru to disciple; in many rituals, it is customary for devotees to bring an offering and to receive prasad in return

Puranas   literally, ancient; a collection of symbolical and allegorical writings, mythological in character; there are 18 such scriptures

raddi   waste material

Ramayana   great epic of Hindu literature; foundation of Indian historical writing, along with the *Puranas* and *Mahabharata*

rishimandal   rishi : sage, mandal : circle; assembly of sages

sadhana   literally, accomplishment; pursuit of an ideal; spiritual practice or discipline

sadhu   literally, good; holy man

sahitya   literature, epic

samadhi   literally, resolution, resolving; "drawing together of the mind" through contemplation, meditation; state of higher consciousness in which the fluctuations of the mind cease

samartha   very capable; capable in all respects

sanatkumar(s)   one of the four sons of Brahma, "the Holy Youths," born of his mind alone

sankalpa   literally, decide to do; a vow or resolution

sanyasi *(sannyasi)*   literally, one who has cast away; a renunciate

Saraswati   (a)goddess of learning and the arts; (b)river;one of three rivers that converge at Allahabad (Saraswati, Jumna, Ganga)

satpurushas   sat : existence, being, purusha : one's true self

satyanarayana   satya : truth; narayana : name of Vishnu; *satyanarayana pooja*   is a popular ritual performed to attain certain desired results

seva   selfless service

shakti   the power of the absolute

Shankara   great Vedantist teacher and author (9th century AD); organized 10 orders of monks and four major monasteries; the chief teacher of each monastery is know as the Shankar/acharya of (city)

shastri   one who is learned in the holy books (shastras)

shishya   disciple

shradda *(shraddha)*   intense faith, deeper than the mind; involves both knowledge and will or dynamism

shuddha bhavana   sincere feeling; purity of feeling and motive

siddhi   literally, accomplishment; any occult power acquired through discipline

stithaprajna   one whose knowledge is firmly established, who is always the witness; who never wavers from consciousness

swami   literally, master of one's Self; title given to monks of the orders organized by Shankara

swaraj   swa : self, raj : kingdom; self-rule, self-government

swayam praapti   self-attained

teerthayatra   pilgrimage

trishula   trident; symbol of the three powers of the absolute: will, knowledge, action; often associated with Shiva

toddy tapper   the sap of the toddy palm is collected and distilled to yield an intoxicating beverage. The person who taps the trees and collects the sap is called a toddy tapper

tonga   horse drawn carriage; still a common mode of travel in rural areas

tulsi   basil

Upanishads   the most recent of the *Vedas*, written about 900 BC (dates disputed); the philosophical portions of the *Vedas*

vairagya   distaste for and detachment from worldly values

Valmiki   author of the *Ramayana*

vasana   literally, smell; predilections, residual traces of actions and impressions retained in the mind; habit energy

veera padmasana   the veera pose is the hero pose, padmasana is the lotus posture

Vedas   oldest scriptures of Hinduism and the most ancient religious texts in an Indo-European language, probably compiled between 1000 - 500 BC (dates disputed)

vishwaroopa   form of the Absolute; universal form of god

walla   suffix meaning "person in charge of, who trades in, who owns"; i.e., the ticketwalla is the person in charge of tickets

yajna   Vedic sacrifice ritual or ceremony

yoga   union of individual self with the Supreme Being or Ultimate Principle; also samadhi or trance

yogi   one who studies and practices yoga

Index